CLACKMANNAN
AND THE OCHILS

AN ILLUSTRATED ARCHITECTURAL GUIDE

I am delighted to have been given the chance to write this foreword. Clackmannanshire and its architecture are too little known. Unlike other parts of central Scotland, it has retained its distinctive character and sense of community.

In retrospect, it is very clear that the publication of the original book 14 years ago was a seminal event for the county. It came at a time when the decline of traditional industries was accelerating and moral was at a very low ebb. The built environment was not normally considered to be of great importance and the quality of many individual buildings and of at least parts of townscapes were seriously underestimated.

In the intervening years, much has been achieved in Clackmannanshire. There are many new buildings of good quality. Of equal importance, is the care which has gone into conserving our architectural heritage. The restoration of Alloa Tower is the flagship project, but many other important schemes have been completed or are in the pipeline.

I am confident that the increased consciousness of local architecture which the book promoted has been an important influence in all of this. This revised edition makes Clackmannanshire's diverse treasures easily accessible and is an indispensable guide to the area's regeneration.

Keir Bloomer
Chief Executive, Clackmannanshire Council

© Author: Adam Swan
Series editor: Charles McKean
Series consultant: David Walker
Editorial consultant: Kate Blackadder
Index: Oula Jones
Cover design: The Almond Consultancy

The Rutland Press
ISBN 1873190530
1st published 1987
2nd edition 2001

Cover illust⸱⸱⸱
Front A⸱⸱⸱
Back C⸱⸱⸱
In⸱⸱⸱

Typesetting and picture scans by
The Almond Consultancy, Edinburgh
Printed by Pillans & Wilson Greenaway, Edinburgh

D1078071

British Library Cataloguing in Publication Data.
A catalogue record for this book is available from the British Library.

Clackmannanshire, Scotland in epitome, historically her smallest county, occupies a small portion of central Scotland on the north banks of the river Forth, populated by under 50,000 persons. Her boundaries are Stirling's huge Abbey Craig rock to the west, the impressive Ochil hills to the north, and Kinross and Fife to the east. The hills and the great river provided barriers which ensured Clackmannanshire's seclusion: the most vital battles in Scots history were fought on her very doorstep, while she offered peaceful retreats to her country's leaders.

An exceptional series of tower houses were occupied by the Bruce, Erskine, Argyll and Schaw families, attendants on the Stuart monarchs at their favoured seat of Stirling. Yet this tiny territory contained other towers and principal residences as well – Hartshaw, Alva, Manor, Menstrie, Tillicoultry, Blairlogie Castle, Glendevon and the Bishop's Palace at Cowden – all but four now vanished. Clackmannanshire lairds were among the first in Scotland to improve and exploit their estates commercially, following the remarkable lead of the 6th Earl of Mar at Alloa, his kinsman Sir John Erskine at Alva and George Abercromby at Tullibody. Coal mines, bleaching greens, mills, canals, breweries and harbours testify to hard-headed practicality, and provided a profitable corrective to Jacobitism. Indeed, the lack of support for the Stuart cause can be inferred from the fact that *the Earl of Mar, with all his popularity, could not raise three men in his own town of Alloa* to support his 1715 rebellion.

Alloa later became one of Britain's first industrial towns and carries the traces of a medium-scale Victorian prosperity. It was too far up the Forth to aspire to greater. Philanthropic burgesses generated grandiose civic buildings, and commissioned opulent and lavishly crafted houses for themselves and their establishments.

The Ochils, extending eastwards from Blairlogie to the Firth of Tay, are most dominant above Clackmannanshire's Hillfoots villages and their omnipresence generates a peculiar loyalty to the settlements on its slopes from their natives. A common characteristic of each of these ancient communities is the 1669 Statute Labour Act Road passing through the upper part of each village. It was superseded by the new Stirling to Kinross turnpike road in 1806 and stretches of it now offer a pleasurable walk. Its existence, however, is a key to understanding the growth of these towns. Blairlogie is Arcadia; Menstrie more

Coal and local wealth were long synonymous. First gathered on the Forth banks by monks, coal was the *raison d'être* for Gartmorn Dam, Sauchie and industrial Alloa. Extracted by the Earls of Mar, Robert Bald, Bruces of Kennet and the Alloa Coal Company, who prospered; speculated on by the Schaws of Sauchie, Bruces of Clackmannan, Erskines of Alva and Taits of Harviestoun, who failed. John Ramsay of Ochtertyre recorded *It is said that Clackmannanshire colliers, in their Litany, used to pray for heavy rains in July, to spoil the west country people's peats*; for the Stirlingshire tenants otherwise relied on Alloa coal for warmth and for fertiliser via their limekilns. Prior to 1900, there were 70 named and about 200 unnamed shafts in the county. By 1946 there were 18. With great optimism, huge new coal pits were opened in the 1950s necessitating the import of complete communities from Lanarkshire, creating the metamorphosis of Tullibody, Sauchie, Coalsnaughton and Fishcross. Their subsequent closure left Clackmannanshire without its oldest indigenous industry and many miners without work.

Opposite: *Solar, Alloa Tower (Bill Robertson).* Below *Ochil hills, Alva.*

Bill Robertson

Top *Garderobe, Clackmannan Tower.* Middle *Conservation in action at Sauchie Tower.* Above *Doorway, Broomhall, Menstrie.*

homespun and slightly schizophrenic; Alva and Tillicoultry are steeped in the heritage of their industrial past; Dollar is an unlikely, classical Enlightenment transplant to Arcadia, now frayed at the edges; while Muckhart's seclusion accounts for the survival of its atmosphere as representing the rural dream. Inexplicably, Rumbling Bridge Gorge has forfeited its fame as a beauty spot, although it retains the beauty and is now more accessible than ever before (unlike neighbouring Cauldron Linn). Glendevon has been included for the pure enjoyment of a remote highland glen so close to industrialised Scotland.

Since the first edition was published 14 years ago some remarkable changes have occurred and, politically, the old county has regained and hung onto its independence, emerging from local government reorganisation as Clackmannanshire once more.

At this guide's launch in July 1987, informal discussions and networking were the catalyst for the late Earl of Mar and Kellie and Clackmannan District Council, guided by architect Bob Heath, determining to resolve the embarrassment that was Alloa Tower. The project-specific Alloa Tower Building Preservation Trust was formed, expertly and imaginatively directed by newly appointed council official Andrew Millar, culminating in the opening of the building in 1997. The trust evolved into Clackmannanshire Heritage Trust and, with the council, has gone on to sort out, one by one, many of Clackmannanshire's outstanding buildings at risk: the Mar and Kellie Mausoleum, the Devon Beam Engine House, Cambus Iron Bridge and, more recently, Sauchie Tower.

About the same time another council initiative resulted in the establishment of Ochil View Housing Association. From small beginnings Ochil View has established a reputation for providing social housing and quality architecture: 20 Mar Street, Broad Street and Bridge Terrace, Alloa, and Mitchell Court, Dollar, being examples of contemporary excellence. The council itself has contributed some good new work, including a programme of refurbishment of local halls – Alloa, Clackmannan, Cochrane, Coalsnaughton, Devonvale – though sadly the interesting corrugated-iron hall at Forestmill has gone. The private sector has been no less responsible: the once ruinous Broomhall above Menstrie is again occupied, the derelict William Stirling designed steading at Tillicoultry and stable block at Alva are now beautifully restored as restaurants (with

the council stepping in as enabler), Dollar has
two excellent contemporary houses as well as
some remarkable additions to its academy, and
Muckhart has been enhanced by the talents of
local architect Matthew Pease.

Inevitably there have also been losses, caused
by the closure of traditional industry, with a
regrettable impact on the local economy. But the
building losses have been minimised. Of the
woollen mill closures, Tillicoultry's Middleton
and Alva's Henry Street mills have been lost but
J & D Patons of Tillicoultry and Alva's Strude Mill
are now flats, Glentana has become a shop and
visitor centre and Clock Mill and Elmbank are
business centres; elsewhere mills have been
replaced by housing. Brunt Mill, Dollar, is now
partly the Dollar Museum. Clackmannanshire
Enterprise has found appropriate new uses for
two of Alloa's best mill-owners' mansions, The
Gean and Inglewood. The companies behind
Alloa Brewery and Thistle Brewery have both
consolidated brewing outwith their historic sites –
and Alloa still brews in a modern industrial
estate. The historically important Thistle Brewery,
along with Paton's Kilncraigs Mills in Alloa and
the long-empty Tullibody Tannery are the three
most significant complexes seeking regeneration –
though the threat of demolition for all is very real,
and has begun at the Tannery. Crying out for the
restoration to its original glory is Alloa's Speirs
Centre – it is among the finest of a diminishing list
of Victorian swimming baths left anywhere.

Top *Mitchell Court, Dollar.* Above *Hall,
Inglewood, Alloa.*

Left *Speirs Centre, former Alloa Public
Baths and Gymnasium c.1900.* Below
Harviestoun Country Inn, Tillicoultry.

River Devon meandering through the Hillfoots.

The River Devon rises behind Alva's Ben Cleuch (the highest Ochil Peak) and, as a gushing stream, winds eastwards through Perthshire's Glendevon until she aptly reaches the Crook of Devon in Kinross-shire. With a sudden turn westwards she changes character, rushing along craggy ravines and tossing through the chasms and falls of Rumbling Bridge gorge and Cauldron Linn (see p.140). Later, more gracious, she meanders through the Hillfoots valley, absorbing each village stream, before encircling Tullibody and slouching into the Forth at Cambus. For a journey of over 30 miles, she is only 5¼ miles from her source.

Organisation of the Guide
This guide opens with a description of Clackmannan, the historic county town, and its hinterland. Alloa is described from the shore to the modern centre, followed by its outer suburbs and the adjoining villages of Sauchie and Fishcross. Thereafter the guide traces the River Devon from outfall to source: from its meeting with the Forth at Cambus near Tullibody, past Blairlogie, Menstrie, Alva, Tillicoultry and Dollar, to Muckhart and nearby beauty spots, up to its source in Glendevon. The best can be explored in a weekend, but it is well worthwhile returning.

Text Arrangement
Entries for principal buildings follow the sequence of name (or number), address, date and architect (if known). Lesser buildings are contained within paragraphs. Both demolished buildings and unrealised projects are included if appropriate. In general, the dates given are those of the design (if known) or of the beginning of construction. Entries in the small column highlight interesting biographical, historical and social aspects of the story of Clackmannanshire.

Map References
Maps are included for the towns and for the Devon Pass, with a larger map covering the county. Numbers do not refer to pages but to the small numbers adjacent to the text itself. Numbers in the index refer to pages.

Access to Properties
The majority of the buildings in this guide are visible from public roads or footpaths. However, only a few of them are normally open for public visiting, and readers are requested to respect the occupiers' privacy. A number of the buildings mentioned offer excellent overnight accommodation and good food and refreshments.

Sponsors
The generous support is gratefully acknowledged of Clackmannanshire Heritage Trust, Clackmannanshire Council, Alloa Library, Argyll, the Isles, Loch Lomond, Stirling & Trossachs Tourist Board, Clackmannanshire Economic Development Partnership, Ochil View Housing Association, Clackmannanshire Enterprise and the Landmark Trust.

Dedication
To the memory of my mother, Sheila Swan.

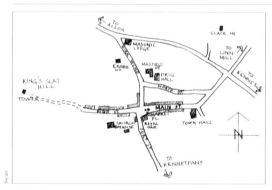

Swan

Below *Clackmannan*. Bottom
*Clackmannan Tower and the parish church
along the ridge of King's Seat Hill.*

CLACKMANNAN

Like Stirling and Edinburgh, Clackmannan is
built with a castle at the high point (King's Seat
Hill to the west) and the town's main street and
market place declining along a ridge to the east.
It commands a superb view over the upper Forth
to Stirling and the Highlands.

The Tower was never a royal fortress. Its early
life as a royal hunting seat ended with its sale to
Robert Bruce in 1359. The town only became a
burgh of barony in the 16th century, by which
time its harbour was silting up and the Bruce
family had lost its national importance, settling
down to its future role as principal landowners in
the area.

Judging from various date stones of houses in
Main Street, the burgh's greatest period was the
late 16th century – the period of the construction
of the tolbooth. In 1772 it remained a *small town
pleasantly situated on a hill,* with a harbour, where
the Black Devon met the Forth (newly improved
by Sir Lawrence Dundas to achieve a mean depth
of 10ft). But the port of Alloa had expanded and
superseded that of Clackmannan. By 1802
Alexander Campbell could record *the wretched
appearance of the houses* which formed *a striking
contrast to the beauty and grandeur of the scenery*

RCAHMS

Stewart Fowler

around it. *Without trade of artificers, this village is fast hastening to decay.* William Chalmers noted the following year that *the town of Clackmannan itself, however, by no means corresponds with the beauty of its situation. The principal street is broad and spacious, but many of the houses are mean and wretched.* A fashionable new parish church in 1815 might be thought to have heralded a revival of some kind. Unfortunately not. The burgh's fine tolbooth and courthouse became *a heap of ruins and a nuisance to the public*, and the sheriff court was transferred to Alloa in 1822. In 1837 Robert Chambers found *an old decayed and deserted town with one long unpaved street*; little improvement was visible 50 years later.

Contemporary Clackmannan differs in that houses have been rebuilt and there are new suburbs. It conveys a slightly eerie sensation of being a town of national potential whose time never came. It is that feeling which makes the trip from the Tower (negotiating barbed wire, cow and dog mess) down to the church and the main street – always with a view over the Forth or north to the Ochils – so worthwhile.

Top *Clackmannan Tower.* Above *Clackmannan Tower with adjoining mansion, 1807.*

Lady Catherine Bruce entertained Robert Burns in September 1787 dressed, it is said, with a tartan scarf and the white rose of the Stuarts. This lady was renowned for conferring the honour of knighthood upon distinguished guests with the great two-handed sword of her ancestor King Robert Bruce. After knighting Burns, her toast was *Hooi uncos,* or *away strangers.*

Clackmannan Tower, from 14th century King's Seat Hill, a spectacular and strategic site in the control of the Forth, was sold with its hunting lodge by King David II to a kinsman, Robert Bruce, in 1359 (possibly to keep it in the family without it continuing a royal burden). The great rectangular tower, of beautifully cut blocks of pink sandstone, was begun soon afterwards to the normal pattern of ground-floor cellars, great hall above, capped by guard house. In the 15th century, a taller square tower, built equally delectably, was added abutting the south, at which time both were presented with a crenellated wallwalk supported on machicolations (open corbels between which defenders could pour unpleasantness upon attackers).

In late 16th century, the Bruces built a splendid mansion block with crowstep gables and turrets to the south west; and in late 17th century, a new entrance court, walled and protected by a moat, to the east, with a new doorway into the tower embellished by a lovely pedimented frame. Fragments of outer walls, garden terrace and ancient bowling green may still be traced.

The main Bruce line died with Lady Catherine Bruce in 1791, soon after which the mansion crumbled and stones were thriftily resetted elsewhere. Tower itself later threatened by coal-mining subsidence. That threat has receded and a major programme of consolidation was announced by Historic Scotland in 2001, with the intention of providing full public access (see p.4).

Doorway detail, Clackmannan Tower.

He who wishes to see things that will shortly be found no more should visit Clackmannan Castle. There he will still find the house, the furniture, and the environs in all the simplicity of former times, yet not without an air of dignity; and what is more rare and precious, he will see in the lady a living specimen of the style and manners of the last age.
John Ramsay of Ochtertyre, MSS

John Ramsay of Ochteryre, 1736–1814, a Stirlingshire landowner, kept diaries concerning many local landed families and their homes, having in particular spent much time in the 1750s with the Abercrombys of Brucefield, Tullibody and Menstrie with whom he had a family connection (also his mother was a Dundas of Manor, west of Tullibody). His manuscripts, written from the 1770s, were published in 1888.

Clackmannan Parish Church.

Clackmannan Parish Church, 1815, James Gillespie Graham
There has been a church or a chapel at Clackmannan since St Serf visited from Culross in the 8th century. The first stone church, consecrated by Bishop David de Bernham of St Andrews in 1249, may have been the one around which the present kirk was constructed. Gillespie Graham was a fashionable choice of architect and he rose to the occasion and fine site, but with a design which he used with subtle differences elsewhere. A delicately detailed, standard Regency box in perpendicular gothic with buttressed tower placed symmetrically against the west gable. Fine plaque by Sir Robert Lorimer

The remarkable floodlighting of Clackmannan Parish Church by Clackmannanshire Heritage Trust was among the most successful of the 1999 Millennium Commission church floodlighting schemes, voted in the top four out of 399 in the UK. Its designer, Kevin Sturrock, was subsequently 'poached' to light Sydney Opera House for the 2000 Olympic Games (colour p.65).

Above *Manse.* Right *44-46 High Street.*

commemorates the Master of Burleigh, who fell at Le Château in 1914, the German wooden cross having been brought from his grave. Kirkyard contains good 17th-, 18th- and 19th-century stones and, unusually, horizontal lying stones. Adjacent **manse**, 1741, one of the larger houses in the town, contains fine Adam-style fireplaces in the public rooms and projecting bay window to catch views to the Forth. Just uphill, mid-19th-century, 1½-storey **Zetland House** also has a fabulous panorama over the Carse.

The end of the 17th century saw the beginning of the decline of the **Bruces** of Clackmannan. From the 1650s Sir Henry Bruce developed the extensive coalfields of Clackmannan, being fortunate in having coal seams near the harbour, but the costs of draining the seams below the level of the Forth and Black Devon were great. Sir Henry spent much time and money trying to solve this problem, building a water-powered *Egyptian Wheel*, an early bucket-and-chain pump. He died in 1674 leaving immense debts to his son, David Bruce. The latter, as well as holding the office of hereditary sheriff, became member of parliament to Charles II and later James VII and II; but by refusing to take the oaths to the government of William and Mary, he was removed in 1693. Meanwhile the collieries were poorly managed and David Bruce was declared bankrupt in 1708. To pay his creditors, he sold the estate and the sheriffdom to Colonel William Dalrymple, second son of the Earl of Stair. David died in Clackmannan in 1712 and his son Henry, 15th Baron of Clackmannan, came out for Prince Charles Edward in the 1745 uprising. He died in 1772, but his widow Catherine Bruce of Newton (b.1696) continued to live in the old mansion and tower until her death in 1791.
The Earl of Elgin, currently head of the Bruce family, is a descendent of the 5th Bruce of Clackmannan. The Kennet Bruces descend from the 8th Baron.

Below *1950s' housing, High Street.* Right *Trade lintel, 4 High Street.*

High Street, 1950s, W H Henry, County Architect
High Street connects the Tower with Market Place, lined on the north by complete row of 18th-century cottages built in rows, blocks and around courtyards, wholly reconstructed in 1950s. The architect re-used many details from the original houses including skewputts, pantiles, corbelled corners of old stonework, date stones and plaques. **No 2** has plaque dated 1702 and two-sided sundial set into a corner stone; **No 4** a lintel dated 1668 and 1738; **Nos 44-46** has scrolled skewputts. At the corner with **Kirk Brae**, two-storey cottage with mullioned and transomed windows, cement render and roof tiles, has thackstanes, crowsteps, skewputts and little outbuildings formed from older cottages in the lee of the Tower. **Kirk Wynd**, **Port Street** and **Garden Place** were rebuilt at the same time, and one corner of Garden Place has an almost identical gable to one in High Street, with uneven skewputts and corbelled stonework. Civic Trust Award, 1959.

Left *The Market Cross and Stone of Mannan in 1861, the original High Street houses are behind.* Above *The same view today.*

Market Place.

Reconstruction drawing of the Tolbooth.

Market Place
Where High Street, descending from the castle, crosses the ancient road from Kincardine to Alloa, it broadens as Market Place, marked by the market cross, the **Stone of Mannan**, and the tower of the ruined Tolbooth. Thence, shaped like a wedge of cheese, it becomes Main Street, narrowing until plugged, like a cork in a bottle, by the 1903 Town Hall at the bottom (colour p.65).

Market Cross, 16th century
Single trefoil shaft, bearing the arms of Bruce at the top. Until the tolbooth was built, prisoners awaiting trial were chained to the cross, the frotting of the chains being the reason for the slenderness of the shaft towards the base.

Tolbooth, from 1592
All that remains is the late 17th-century belfry tower. William Menteith, Sheriff of Clackmannan, presented a petition to parliament requesting that a tolbooth be built, since he and his predecessors had *been compelled to hold courts open at the Market Cross of Clackmannan … and keep inward the transgressors and malefactors within his dwelling house.* An Act was duly passed authorising its construction and the gathering of taxes *to the sum of twa hundred fourscore and four punds.* The bell, presented by Sir Lawrence Dundas in 1765, was

David Lowthian stole six shirts belonging to the Countess of Dumfries (wife of Colonel William Dalrymple, the laird), and his sister Jean resetted some of them, the stolen goods being found in the custody of David's wife, Elizabeth Reid. David and Jean were sentenced in 1733 to be *scourged by the hands of a hangman from the head to the foot of the town of Clackmannan,* this treatment to be repeated after a stay in the tolbooth and *thereafter to be burned upon the cheek with a mark of the shire, and the said David and Jean Lowthian and the said Elizabeth Reid to be banished the shire and never to return again thereafter.*

rung each evening at 6pm until 1939. By 1803, tolbooth and courthouse had become that *heap of ruins and a nuisance to the public,* and was wholly abandoned by 1822. Now requires sensitive repair (colour p.66).

Right 2 Main Street. *Below* Town Hall.

The name **Clackmannan** is derived from *Clack* signifying stone, church or village, and *Mannan,* an ancient district of Scotland around the head of the River Forth. The *Stone of Mannan* was worshipped by ancient pagans who believed it contained the spirit of the sea-god *Manau.* Its original position was at Lookaboutye Brae, probably once the shore of the Forth. Later it was brought to the centre of the burgh and, in 1833, raised onto a whinstone plinth which was dragged from the Abbey Craig at Stirling by Bruce of Kennet and 16 stout horses.

The credulous enjoy an alternative explanation of the name and of the county motto 'Look about ye'. King Robert Bruce had been hunting in the Forest of Clackmannan, and on returning to the tower discovered that he had lost his glove. With the instruction *Look about ye,* he sent his followers to search for the glove (*mannan*), which was found by the stone (*clack*) on the brae (*Lookaboutye Brae*) to the south of the town.

Main Street contains some fine 18th- and 19th-century houses, several converted to shops, some with interesting wrought-iron gutter brackets. Curved gable of housing at **No 2**, former Royal Oak Hotel, *c.*1700, recalls Clackmannanshire's extensive trade with the Low Countries, the name itself that of a locally owned 18th-century ship, a painting of which once hung in the Tower. Gap sites on both sides, about halfway along, were infilled with suitable houses in 1970 by W H Henry. Cottages on the south side have a pend leading through to similar housing at Garden Place. The 1992 date on the two-storey house opposite refers to its reconstruction.

Town Hall, 1903, Ebenezer Simpson
Art Nouveau red sandstone two-storey block closing Main Street gifted by John Thomson-Paton to provide library, billiards and reading rooms in front of the 1888 Town Hall by Adam Frame. Double and triple gothic windows have transoms, a pedimented crest frowns over the entrance and there is Art Nouveau lettering and sculptured architraves. Four rainwater heads between the windows are decorated with animals. Upgraded and extended with 1993 **Community Access Point** extension, which neatly picks up the rhythm and colour of the façade, turning the corner into Cattlemarket, but keeps the scale of surrounding cottages leaving original building dominant.

Little historic remains in **North Street**, except the odd stone warehouse, although scale is light and airy. Front part of **Drill Hall** was once the *Penny School* of Clackmannan, each pupil contributing one penny towards their education. **Mayfield House**, 1862, John Melvin, at the corner of Kirk Wynd, is a simple classical bay-fronted house built as the manse of the Free (Mayfield) Church.

Kirk Wynd forms northern wing of the historic Alloa to Kincardine road, with two Secession churches: the Relief Church, founded in 1788 following dissatisfaction by the parish with their minister, and the Free Church built after the Disruption in 1843. Both abandoned at the Triple Union in 1932: the Relief demolished in 1933, and the Free, one of a series designed locally, 1845, by John Burnet, is now the **Masonic Lodge**. Street name is appropriate, but in fact an early resident was named Kirk. **Erskine House**, c.1830, former Relief Manse, delightful two-storey classical house with pilastered door and architraves above ground-floor windows, set in large high-walled garden.

Masonic Lodge.

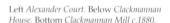

Left *Alexander Court.* Below *Clackmannan House.* Bottom *Clackmannan Mill c.1880.*

Alexander Court, Mill Road, 1990, by Carronvale Building Company, a pleasant little grouping of single-storey reproduction vernacular cottages, with multi-pane windows, white wetdash render, pantiled roofs and stone quoins and skews. Next door, **Clackmannan House**, c.1815, classical two-storey house with basement and attic. There is a fine doorway, with Tuscan columns, pilasters and fanlight, in a ground floor of rusticated grey freestone. All surrounded by less successful modern housing – on the site of Paton's Clackmannan Mill. **Mill Villa**, 19th-century, two-storey, double house, with arched windows above the central doors and very decorative gothic mouldings.

With the demolition of Paton's **Clackmannan Mill** in 1983 – a 1875 outpost of their Kilncraig's Mill in Alloa – former **Clackmannan Public School**, Alloa Road, c.1910, dominates the south edge of town. Sadly, boarded and smashed windows indicate it is at serious risk.

Clackmannan Colliery

From the 1650s the carselands between Clackmannan and the Forth were explored for coal by Sir Henry Bruce. William Dalrymple, who came into possession in 1708, provided the colliery with a water-powered drainage wheel and lined the Pow (port) at the mouth of the Black Devon with stone blocks to improve the landing place for loading coal into flat-bottomed boats. After 1742, Sir Laurence Dundas of Kerse, the next owner (whose family became Marquises of Zetland), built a sea wall from the Pow down to Kennetpans where there was a more substantial harbour. In 1770 he constructed a wagon road from his mines to Kennetpans, rebuilt the harbour and straightened the course of Black Devon itself two years later. Little now remains. **Craigie Farm** is on the location of the main pit, the Speedwell pit being further west. The old lade which served the water wheels at these pits can still be made out in places (colour p.65).

Right *Kennet House*. Below *Kennet Lodge*.

Kennet.

I was one week at Kennet where I spent my time very pleasantly – no appearance of famine or straits there. A very pleasant house were they a little further from the coals; but they are mending in that respect.
John Ramsay of Ochtertyre, *Letters*

Inch of Ferryton marks the site of what was once probably an island on the Forth, at the ferry crossing point to Dunmore on the opposite bank. The Stone of Mannan may once have rested here before being moved first to **Lookaboutye Brae**, on the old road out of Clackmannan, and to its present site.

Kennet House, *c.*1795, Thomas Harrison
Built on much older site *in a style of elegance and simplicity that marks the taste and judgement of the owner* (Alexander Bruce of Kennet), this classical mansion, with side wings, its bowed Tuscan porch answering its segment-headed, Tuscan-columned tripartite windows, was *situated amid pleasure gardens and plantations of great beauty, on a rising ground overlooking the basin of the Forth*. The Kennet Bruces, by then Balfours of Burleigh, sold Kennet to Alloa Co-operative Society in 1946 for subdivision into flats and restored Brucefield House as their main residence. Sold again and demolished by the army in 1968. Delightful tiny bow-fronted **Kennet Lodge** still marks entrance to a long, curving avenue.

KENNET

Complete row of 20 *c.*1800 miners' cottages (No 3 dated 1804) built by the Bruce family for miners at Kennet Colliery. Well built of cut stone, with pantiled roofs, the cottages were restored, early 1980s, by Clackmannan District Council, as fine example of an 18th-century miners' row.

KENNETPANS

Formerly a salt-panning community on the Forth. In medieval times salt was mainly used for preserving food for winter, and the first panning was undertaken by small communities of monks, evaporating water from the salt in large cast-iron pans over coal-fired furnaces. The practice continued until late 18th century.

Kennetpans House, 1783
Only the walled kitchen garden survives of John Stein's mansion: the lawns now marshy wasteland. **Broadcarse Farmhouse**, nearby, late 18th-century two-storey farm with symmetrically planned side wings. Recently restored after long period of dereliction.

Left Distillery ruins at Kennetpans. Top Section drawing of The Garlet. Above The Garlet c.1930.

The Garlet, near Kilbagie, remodelled 1670 (demolished c.1965)
Second house to Kennet, often occupied by younger sons, let to the Erskines in 1629, but granted to a second son by Robert Bruce around or before 1642 and again, by another Robert Bruce, to his son Alexander in 1670 (Alexander died in Ireland in 1704). Probably remodelled for another Bruce after 1704, and was an attractive small mansion with crowsteps, pantiles and quoins, distinguished by projecting entrance gable at the centre of the façade with pilastered entrance, heraldic panel and round attic window.

KILBAGIE
Site of the Steins' principal distillery before 1776, which, at its peak, produced more than 3,000 tons of spirit annually from over 60,000 bolls of grain. The *draff or* waste grain fed 7,000 cattle and 2,000 pigs. Distillery buildings covered over three acres of ground and employed more than 300 men. By 1795 the distillery had been sold by James Stein's creditors for under one fifth of its cost, but that family was in business again at Kilbagie in the early 1800s. The spirit was shipped from Kennetpans (then a free port) and transported to the harbour along a canal, now known as Canal Burn. Distillery survived until mid-19th century, became a chemical plant for a short period, before being put to its present use as a paper mill.

The Garlet was the birthplace of Mary Erskine, 1629–1707, a pioneer of education for girls. A successful private banker in Edinburgh, she contributed to the setting up of the Merchant Maiden Hospital in 1694 to which she also bequeathed 10,000 merks Scots. The hospital became a day school for girls, known as Edinburgh Ladies' College, in 1869, before changing its name to Mary Erskine's School in 1944.

By the 1770s James and John Stein, farmers on the Kennet estate, had established distilleries at Kennetpans and Kilbagie, using local grain and fuel to produce gin for London, shipped from Kennetpans harbour. Their distilleries proved so successful that London rivals sought to put them out of business. In the 1780s, laws were passed to increase the taxation on spirits produced in Scotland. By 1790 the yearly taxation per gallon of every still was 2/6d in England, while in Scotland it had risen to a staggering £9 sterling. Before these new taxes were enforced, the two distilleries contributed more money in taxation to the government than all the Scottish land tax. Fascinating ruins remain today.

Kilbagie Mills, 1874 and earlier
Converted to paper mill by J A Weir Ltd, and still operated by the Inveresk Group, some 18th-century, rubble-built distillery buildings survive. Complex dominated by huge rectangular brick water tower. **Kilbagie House**, *c.*1776, fairly plain dwelling of James Stein and now Inveresk Group offices, sits above the mill buildings, decorated with single attic porthole, moulded doorways and club skewputts. West addition, *c.*1800, bow fronted with shaped gable. Behind, walled courtyard with outbuildings and nearby rusticated gatepiers.

Tulliallan and **Kincardine on Forth**
See *The Kingdom of Fife* in this series.

Linn Mill
Site (since 1690) of two ancient grain mills on the Black Devon, near Grassmainston Farm, now surviving only as group of small 18th-century cottages next to high arched bridge; west-most one being archetype of the traditional **cottage** – two small windows, centre door, crowstepped gable and pantiled roof.

From top *Kilbagie Mills by Adam Robson; Kilbagie House; Mill House, Kilbagie, mid-18th-century harled house, now offices; Cottage, Linn Mill.* Right *Cast-iron sluice gate at Forestmill.*

Forestmill was originally a hamlet, or fermtoun, of a grain mill, on the Black Devon within Clackmannan Forest. In 1766 the teacher at the local school was Michael Bruce, author of the poem *Lochleven.* Bruce, a weaver's son, died penniless the following year, aged 21, and his poems gained popularity when published in 1770.

Water for Gartmorn Dam is drawn off the Black Devon along a lade just south of the village; large weir and sluice gates, early 18th century.

Stewart Fowler

Brucefield House (colour p.66)

Rebuilt 1714 and renamed by Alexander Bruce (the younger) of Kennet, incorporating older house, probably of Hartshaw, 15th-century hunting lodge of the Stewarts of Rosyth. Evidence of this older house as a small tower with a turnpike stair within the walls; tower had a palace block and service corridor added to north east. Cellars taken out and replaced with columns, and new stair added to east, possibly *c*.1690. Alexander Bruce's contribution was probably to remodel and extend the tower, encase its stairtower and to add the balancing south wing, making his *new place at Brucefield* look like a smaller, smarter version of Tullibody House. Slate roofs are hipped and steeply pitched, with tall prominent chimneystacks in the manner of grand early country houses of Scotland. Entrance, now through Doric-columned porchway on west front, formerly at first-floor level on east front, commemorated by a window. Beautifully restored *c*.1936–58, after long period of neglect, by James Shearer, with good period woodwork. **Stable block** of Brucefield Mains, early 18th century, very pleasing open square, white harled with pantiled roofs, with re-used armorial stone, presumably from Hartshaw.

Hartshaw Farm near Brucefield, 18th century, U-shaped whitewashed cottage, with pantiles and gabled attic dormers. Nearby pantiled **Hartshaw Mill**, built as corn mill early 1700s, now used for storage. Cottage's west wing has inscribed stone initialled ROS, dated 1574, probably recording work to Hartshaw.

Clackmannanshire Council

Brucefield House.

Andrew Meikle, an Alloa engineer, invented a threshing machine which was first constructed by his son George, at Kilbagie in 1787. It consisted of a simple device of rollers, one equipped with blades, which removed the grain from the straw mechanically, the grain falling through a mesh and the straw being pulled out of the machine by another roller.

About 1724, Alexander Bruce of Kennet … set about making a new place at Brucefield. It was seemingly a wild undertaking to set down a house upon the top of a moor without a tree. The want of natural beauties was the most striking for its being so near a rich variegated country … In the garden … the last Kennet used to raise the earliest and best kitchen crops in the country … It may, however, be questioned whether the family gained essentially by making Brucefield. The same money and attention bestowed upon their old seat three score years ago, would have made a far better return … About the year 1758 or 1759 Lord Kennet sold Brucefield to the late James [Abercromby – possibly meaning George]. The very name 'Brucefield' was new, it being part of the barony of Hartshaw, which belonged to a family of Stewarts.
John Ramsay of Ochtertyre, MSS

Brucefield was later bought back by the Bruces and is currently home to Robert Bruce, Lord Balfour of Burleigh (a forfeited title restored to the Kennet Bruces following their successful 1868 claim).

Alexander Campbell, wrote in 1802, after the death of both George and Ralph Abercromby that: *Brucefield, the residence of Sir Ralph Abercromby's father, has nothing either of convenience, or ornament to recommend it to notice.*

When his father retired to Brucefield, Sir Ralph (and Lady) Abercromby moved up to Tullibody House; not a good move, according to contemporary commentators: *From the time of their marriage they had lived at Menstry, a place of great capacity, where the same money laid out in policy would have gone three times further than in the carse. Some people, therefore, think it ought to have been the family seat.*
John Ramsay of Ochtertyre, MSS

Stable block, Brucefield Mains.

Alloa in 1672, drawn by Captain John Slezer.

From the time of their arrival in Alloa in the 14th century, the **Erskines of Mar** played a major role in the history of Scotland. For loyalty to David II, Sir and Dumbarton; the present Earl of Mar and Kellie is still hereditary keeper of Stirling Castle. The 3rd Lord Erskine was made responsible for the safety Robert Erskine was appointed Keeper of the royal castles of Stirling, Edinburgh of the young James V (Stirling Castle being chosen as the safest retreat) after the fall of James IV at Flodden (1513). For six years the young Mary Queen of Scots resided with the Erskine family, before being taken to France. It was at Alloa House that Queen Mary reconciled with Darnley when she granted the 5th Lord the long-sought title of Earl of Mar, one month before her wedding in 1565.

One tradition holds that while Mary was visiting Alloa at a later date her infant son died, and it was a substituted infant of the Earl of Mar who was to become James VI and I: a tradition reinforced by the strong facial likeness of the Stuarts to the Erskines.

The last Earl of Mar had a great turn for architecture and was always ready to give his neighbours advice. Tullibody, Tillicoultry and Blairdrummond Houses are said to have been built upon his plans. The Rebellion of 1715 broke out ere his additions to Alloa House were finished.
John Ramsay of Ochtertyre, MSS

1 **Alloa Tower**, from 14th century (colour p.67)
Alloa Tower, one of the largest in Scotland, was the home of one of the country's most distinguished families – the Erskines, Earls of Mar. The Tower is all that remains of a grand complex. The **great house**, adjoining the Tower, *sumptuously furnished* according to Sir Robert Sibbald in 1692, was burnt in 1800 with grievous loss of historic portraits and furnishings. Its successor, a classical mansion, 1834–8, by George Angus, much Victorianised in Tudor style, *c.*1866, by John Melvin, following another fire, was demolished in 1959.

The Erskines were granted Alloa as their principal seat in 1363, and the great Tower and associated defences must already have been long complete by the time of the first reference to a *Manor or Castle* at Alloa in a 1497 charter. Its current curious appearance is the result of rows of 18th-century windows punched through 11 feet of wall, and the wallwalk and roundels. Prior to improvements, the Tower consisted of a Great Hall, private apartments above and guardroom in the roof space, all connected by turnpike stair in the thickness of the south-west corner, still lit by original slit windows. Parapet lowered (probably by Mar during his work on the house), but bartizans original. In 1618 Taylor the Water Poet *saw the outside of a faire and stately house called Alloway, belonging to the Earle of Marr.*

The Erskines of Mar were great improvers, and had not the estates been forfeited after the 1715 rebellion, the history of Alloa could have been significantly different. Improvements to the Tower were in hand by 1672 (there is an account of the house adjoining to the east being destroyed by fire around this time) when it was sketched by Captain John Slezer. Slezer's drawing shows the tower with a great courtyard of tall buildings to the east, and older ones to the south, clearly meriting the praise lavished upon it by travellers during the 18th century.

Clackmannanshire Council

Left 1780s' engraving of the great house from the south. What had been built of the baroque ornamentation did not survive for long.

In early 1700s, the 6th Earl began a programme of extraordinary alterations. At least one smaller *old tower* was demolished and the court on the town side redesigned to give open forecourt facing the entrance. Within, the structure of first floor was removed (put back early 19th century) and magnificent semicircular, domed staircase, cut out of wall thickness, opened onto gallery round three sides of the room at present first-floor level. Unfortunately, reinstated floor spoils impressive sweep of the stairs and blocks the view of the double apartment. A truly baroque conception of space and light giving a sense of monumental grandeur. At the same time, main door (main entrance from medieval times) enriched by Ionic pilasters, pediment and sculpted Erskine crest and motto *Je pense plus*, all almost certainly designed by Mar, though Mar's drawing shows double doors with niche between, and carving (apart from pilaster pedestals) all appears to have been replaced in the 19th century.

Difficult, now, to form a picture of the extensive pleasure grounds Mar designed and constructed round the tower from late 1702 until his exile in 1716 (colour p.68). The plan was inspired by the formal gardens of Louis XIV's gardener Le Nôtre and Mar was assisted by the landscape designer, Alexander Edward, who brought back a large collection of plans from his travels. However, Mar may have already possessed a plan of Le Nôtre's Versailles, as he had begun the great avenue south

Daniel Defoe, in 1723, thought the *Castle of Alloway ... is now so beautify'd, the buildings, and especially the gardens, so compleat and compleatly modern, that no appearance of a castle can be said to remain ... The gardens of Alloway House, indeed, well deserve a description; they are, by much, the finest in Scotland, and not outdone by many in England; the gardens, singly describ'd, take up above forty acres of ground, and the adjoining wood, which is adapted to the house in avenues and vistas, above three times as much.*

He proceeded upon a great scale. His gardens at Alloa were in the Dutch taste, on the model of Hampton Court, the favourite residence of King William. They were nicely kept, a master gardener and twelve men being constantly employed till after the forfeiture. But though much visited and admired they were too magnificent and expensive to be imitated by the country gentlemen of those times. By their means, perhaps the rearing and trimming of hedges was first introduced among us.
John Ramsay of Ochtertyre, MSS

Left The 7th Earl of Mar and family, 1783, by David Allan. The eldest son was painted out and replaced by the top hat in the tree after a family disagreement. Below Alloa Tower in 1788 by David Allan. Part of the great house can be seen behind.

National Galleries of Scotland / Earl of Mar and Kellie

RCAHMS

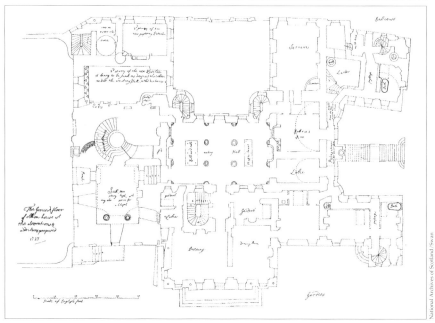

National Archives of Scotland / Swan

Ground-floor plans of the Earl's additions, 1727. The tower became a chapel, other features included a waiting hall with shuffleboard and billiard table, pully chairs or lifts, bathrooms, the two-storey Great Sallon, and a reservoir on the roof which also powered the fountains in the garden.

The Earl of Mar's additions to Alloa Tower, designed in 1727: the finest baroque palace in Scotland. South-west and north-east elevations.

National Archives of Scotland (RHP 13258/13&15)

through the parks before Edward arrived in 1702. Formal layout of planned vistas earned it Pennant's description of *extensive gardens planted in the old style* consisting of *long avenues, clipped hedges, statues and ornaments.* Mar was credited by the Earl of Haddington as the man who introduced the *Wilderness way of planting* into Scotland.

Restoration by Bob Heath and Martin Hadlington for Alloa Tower Building Preservation Trust (now Clackmannanshire Heritage Trust) began in 1988 with the philosophy of retaining historic fabric through honest repairs and use of traditional materials (see p.2). Major work was retention and repair, led by structural engineer Ted Ruddock, of original medieval oak roof. Discoveries during works included 17th-century wallpaper, cellar under main stairs and medieval well with first-floor access – unique in Scotland. Removal of plaster ceiling in the **Charter Room** on the second floor revealed two groin-vaulted stone ceilings – the one above the dome now also visible through an inspection hatch. Landscape research by Margaret Stewart indicates the planned landscape really did exist and features have been identified. Result is that five acres of gardens round the Tower have been recreated by Gordon Haynes to a primacy date of *c.*1710, steadily maturing.

Culmination of restoration was official opening in July 1997 by Her Majesty Queen Elizabeth. Tower provides a facility for local functions and a

Alloa Tower.

The 6th Earl of Mar, 1675–1732, became the father of industrial Alloa by his development of the harbour, Customs House, coal mines and the construction of Gartmorn Dam to provide water power to drain the mines. The dam's water powered the drive shaft of Alloa's industry (now contaminated by open-cast mines). Secretary of State for Scotland to Queen Anne, Mar was dismissed under suspicion for Jacobitism by the Hanoverians. He returned to Scotland and became Commander-in-Chief to 'James VIII', ineptly leading the Jacobite forces at the ill-fated Battle of Sheriffmuir in 1715. He went into exile and died impoverished at Aix-la-Chapelle (now Aachen, Germany) in 1732. His forfeited estates were bought by his brother Lord Grange who restored them to the family.

From his exile, the Earl restlessly planned and redesigned his estates, Stirling Castle, houses in France and, so his sketch books reveal, plans for a new town at Edinburgh and a Forth and Clyde Canal.

return home for the Earl of Mar and Kellie's magnificent collection of David Allan landscapes and portraits, and other furnishings. Many awards include 1994 RTPI Commendation, Patrick Geddes Saltire Society Award and a much-coveted 1999 Civic Trust Award.

Administered by National Trust for Scotland; open for visitors in summer

Tower Square, 1852, former stable block, 2 characterised by tower above northern arched entrance, a pleasant two-storey courtyard. Restored and converted to housing, 1994, Bob Heath and Ochil View Housing Association in association with Alloa Tower Building Preservation Trust (colour p.67).

To the south, Scotland's first combined respite and care facility for dementia sufferers, with amenity housing, 1990, Wheeler and Sproson. 3 Further east, on site of Alloa House, **Burleigh Way**, 1989, James F Stephen, was Ochil View Housing Association's first scheme and re-uses a stone armorial panel from the demolished house.

However blamable the last Earl of Mar might be as a statesman and general he falls to be considered as a pattern for a great man who wishes to establish a family interest founded on the good will and affection of his neighbours. He was always ready to serve (his neighbours) in small as well as in great matters without seeming to expect anything in return and his manners were uniformly gracious and easy at home and abroad. John Ramsay of Ochtertyre, MSS

Left *Tower Square.* Below *Charter Room, Alloa Tower.*

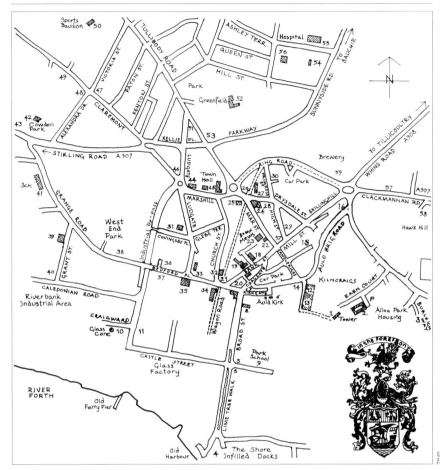

James Sligo Jameson, 1856–88, naturalist and explorer was born at the Walk House, Lime Tree Walk. His family had been sheriff clerks since 1765. Aged 21, James visited Borneo, the Kalahari Desert and then on to explore Kipling's *great grey-green greasy Limpopo River*. Trips to Spain and Algeria followed. In 1887 he joined H M Stanley's controversial Congo expedition, from which he sent home authoritative papers, before succumbing to a fever.

View from Alloa across the Forth c.1900.

4 The Shore

It is almost impossible, now, to appreciate the importance of Alloa's harbour and ferry to its growth as an 18th-century industrial town. First mentioned in 1502, the harbour expanded in importance with the arrival in 1710 of the Customs House, responsible for all upper Forth ports. Defoe found a good harbour, 13 years later, wherein the Glasgow merchants were proposing to erect export warehouses for tobacco and sugar. In 1772, Pennant found the harbour exporting

over one third of Scotland's total coal production, and by 1800 it was handling 7,241 tons of shipping each year, employing 500 seamen. The harbour was attractive to traders for its rough-hewn stone quay, double tide and safe anchorage. Four years later, during the Napoleonic wars, it was noted, approvingly, as being able to take warships of up to 40 guns. In 1803 Chalmers commented that: *The situation of the town is uncommonly beautiful; and its harbour is very commodious, receiving vessels of the greatest burden. It is a place of considerable trade, and shipping. An excellent dry dock has been lately erected; and Alloa has long been famous for building ships.*

The successful harbour brought industry (in 1843 there were proposals to bridge the Forth at this point) and soon it was handling 2,000 vessels a year. In 1878 the Caledonian Railway Company proposed a railway bridge (somewhat resembling the already ill-fated first Tay Bridge) from Alloa (upstream of the harbour) to Falkirk, via south Alloa on the far side of the Forth, opened in 1885 and one of nine local railway bridges dismantled from 1978. A steam crane lifted railway trucks from the rails and tipped coal into boats alongside the quay (scrapped *c.*1940). Silting and relative isolation made the harbour vulnerable to faster methods of transport; the Alloa ferry ceased in 1937 and only the occasional ship visited to unload sand from Holland for the glassworks. Infilled, 1950s, before growth of leisure and tourism indicated a better alternative future.

Lime Tree Walk

Formed by the Earl of Mar as formal route from Alloa to the harbour, very similar to a comparable walk between Dundee and its harbour (see *Dundee* in this series). Upper end, originally called John's Street and latterly Broad Street, planned by Mar as eastern flank of a new town. Of this fine promenade, nothing original survives. Defoe found Lime Tree Walk *a very spacious, well built street, with rows of trees finely planted all the way*, so much so he took it for the High Street of Alloa – as maybe Mar intended it to be. Limes and spaciousness survive, in altered but recoverable circumstances. Only built survivals are extraordinary **gatepiers** to the pleasure grounds, erected 1714. Outer piers have quatrefoil plan, topped with tall pyramidal finials set on balls. Inner piers probably built 1838. Huge potential to recreate to the scale of the original Lime Tree Walk and Broad Street buildings.

The Dry Dock at Alloa by David Allan, 1791, showing the Tower and Wagon Road with James Allan and John Francis Erskine.

David Allan, 1744–96, son of the Alloa harbour master, was brought up at the Shore. His artistic talents came to the notice of Lady Cathcart of Schawpark and she, with her friends Mrs Abercromby of Tullibody and Lady Frances Erskine, sponsored him at art schools in Glasgow and Rome, where he was the first Scotsman to be awarded the gold medal for historical composition. Allan wrote to Lady Erskine in 1773: *Former favours I have already received naturally invites me to send something to Alloa in my way of painting, and write that I am well and never forget the generous assistance which my benefactor has been pleased to grant in placing me in this first and noblest school in Rome.*

Gatepier, Lime Tree Walk.

Thomas Tucker, reporting to Oliver Cromwell of a visit to Alloa in 1655: *On the north side of the Firth, there is a pretty fine burgh called Alloway, having a fine harbour, and an excellent coale, which for the most part is shipped out and carryed away by the Dutch, there being noe vessell belonging to the place … The towne of Kennet, likewise, is a very good greate coale, but chiefly sent from port to port, and never seldome outwards.*

Wagon Road, 1768

Coal from Sauchie was pulled by ponies in wagons or carts with cast-iron wheels, three at a time, along a wagon road which ended at Alloa Harbour (later continued to the glassworks and extended as far as Devon Colliery as a tramway running on narrow gauge rails). Parts survive as footpath between Primrose Street and the former Burgh School, with brick arches under the streets.

Old Town of Alloa

The town is pleasant, well built, and full of trade, recorded Daniel Defoe in 1723, *at Alloway a merchant may trade to all parts of the world.* Full of trade indeed, for it had little other claim to fame; the heart of the old parish being Tullibody to the west, and the town only a burgh of barony. It was thus the creature of the energetic feu superiors, the Earls of Mar, who had a vested interest in promulgating trade. That being Alloa's *raison d'être,* its subsequent history should raise no eyebrows: for, with the exception of two buildings, the entire old town of Alloa, with its **market place**, lies beneath and within the fief of Paton's Kilncraigs Mill and Candleriggs car park, and Maclay's Brewery.

By the close of the 17th century it consisted of a few narrow streets and Market Place, by the bridge over the Brathie (or Brothie) Burn: but the burn was also the means of powering industry, and in a conflict between the old town of Alloa and industry, industry always won. In the 18th century, some southern properties were demolished for extensions to Alloa House

Top *Old Market Place c.1870, now under Paton's Mills. The land on the left, c.1700, was the Speaker's Lodgings.* Above *Auld Brig c.1900.*

pleasure grounds and, to compensate, the
Erskines feued to the west (Forth Street, from
1785) and to the north (Mar Street). The main
road to Clackmannan was re-aligned to the north
and now comprises the town's commercial spine
of Shillinghill, Mill Street and Bank Street.

By 1800 the town was busily engaged in
making *glass bottles, bricks, tiles, tanning, tobacco
manufacture, camblets, broad cloth, linen, muslin,
iron works and coal export*, particular attention
being drawn to the *ingenious family of Meikles,
engineers and millwrights, well known for their
inventions*, who had long settled there. Indeed,
the town was possibly more prosperous in 1750
than 50 years later, only picking up population
again *c*.1840. By then, the new streets were
welcomed for their *neat appearance*, but the old
ones dismissed as *narrow and irregular*. In 1861
Lothian commented *Even our Old Town has of late
years undergone a marked change for the better –
thanks chiefly to the enterprise of private business
firms which, with a view to the extension of their
establishments, have bought up and swept away whole
tenements of dilapidated dwelling-houses, and planted
in their room more enduring and useful buildings.*
There was thus no objection when the old Market
Place was obliterated in 1868 by Paton's
Kilncraigs Mill; **Auld Brig** over Brathie Burn – a
haunt of poor repute – soon followed, the burn
now culverted beneath Kilncraigs Mill site.

Modern Alloa is a post-Enlightenment,
industrial creation, some old street names
surviving around Candleriggs car park – Old High
Street, Old Bridge Street, Kirkgate, Greenside
Street and New Entry. Now that Younger's of
Alloa, with its India Export, has vanished like
Market Place, and demolition faces Paton's and
Maclay's, it is time for a post-industrial recreation
of the Old Town which Clackmannanshire Council
is taking steps to secure through its Old Alloa
Townscape Heritage Initiative.

6 **Old Kirk**, 1680, John Buchanan, Tobias Bauchop
and Pat Main
Only ruined west gable and bell tower of old
Parish Church of St Mungo remain. Walls of
church were ashlar, gable and lower tower rubble
and top stages ashlar, beneath delightful bell-
shaped roof. Original kirk in existence by 1401, as
a chapel of the church of Clackmannan, not
united with Tullibody as a separate parish until
1600. Almost totally rebuilt, 1680, with additional
Mar Aisle to the north. Tower shows great
similarities to ruined tolbooth tower in

Top *Auld Brig c.1920.* Above *Old Kirk.*

According to **John Crawford**, the
Archbishop of St Andrews' warrant and
specifications for rebuilding the Auld
Kirk required: *Imp. of hewen stones, 4000
pieces; item of wall stones, 3000 carts; item
of lime, 50 chalders; item of sand, 600 carts.*
The *slater*, William Bow of Airth,
required 19,500 *skeilie* (slates) for the
roof and 2000 for the steeple. It was to
cost *two thousand and an hundred merks
scotes ... but the workmen have designed
two entries, after the dorrick order, with an
embosement on the front, which, if they be
perfected as they ought, cannot be done for
under five hundred merks scots.*

Clackmannan. Niche in surviving gable houses statue of St Mungo. Church condemned as unsafe, 1816, and stones used in construction of new church in Bedford Place. Extensive re-roofing works to belfry carried out, 1982, by Clackmannan District Council (colour p.69).

Spacious kirkyard, dominated by Paton's Mill, contains fine 18th-century memorials within its high rubble walls.

Mar and Kellie Mausoleum, Kirkgate, 1819, James Gillespie Graham

Built by the architect of the new parish church in the same year, on the site of the old Mar Aisle, the mausoleum is a delicate gothic rectangle containing memorials to the Mar family from 16th century. Splendid groin-vaulted plaster ceiling once decorated with flower paintings and rococo panels. Restoration, 1994, Bob Heath, for Clackmannanshire Heritage Trust, successfully saved the building, though the details must wait for future investment (colour p.69).

Top *Date stone, Kirkgate.* Above *Mar and Kellie Mausoleum.* Right *Bauchop's House.*

Tobias Bauchop (or Baak), died 1710, was the most accomplished member of a family of outstanding stone masons and architects working in the area at the close of the 17th century. Tobias reconstructed Alloa Kirk in 1680 and Logie Kirk in 1684 (the year he married there *by order from the Bishop of Edinburgh,* Margaret Lindsay, *ane womane of ye barbarous perjured ceremonymongers,* having – according to Crawford – *left the kirk of his forbears),* becoming Master Mason to Sir William Bruce, pioneer of Scottish Classicism. He was employed at Bruce's own Kinross House (from 1687 – see *Perth & Kinross* in this series) and later at Hopetoun House, Craigiehall and Mertoun. Bauchop is best remembered for his Dumfries Town House (see *Dumfries and Galloway* in this series) built in 1705, for which his clients called him architect.

Kirkgate c.1900.

7 **Bauchop's House**, 25 Kirkgate, 1695, Tobias Bauchop (colour p.69)

Finest town house in Clackmannanshire, in finely pointed ashlar – *that most aristocratic looking tenement on the north side of Kirkgate* (Crawford). Carved stonework is of magnificent quality. Openings have delicate moulded architraves with lugs. Above doorway is a garlanded shield with initials TB and ML and 1695 – Tobias Bauchop and Margaret Lindsay – and finely carved sundial supported by (again according to Crawford) *the only authentic petrified portrait of Auld Nick in existence.* Frontage restored, 1979, with help from National Trust for Scotland and Clackmannan District Council, but more work required.

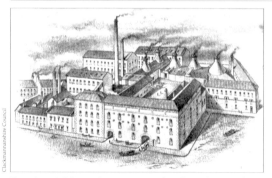

Bauchop's House long sat out the demolition of surrounding houses and then industry in isolation, eventually joined by the new flats opposite in **Kirkgate**, 1986, Clackmannan District Council Architects, in a graceful rhythm of pink tinted blockwork. These coincidentally replicate the scale of previous houses. Future development planned to enclose Kirkgate again, as part of Clackmannanshire Council's Heritage Lottery Fund sponsored Old Alloa Townscape Heritage Initiative project. Traditional proportioned rendered houses by James F Stephen will surround Bauchop's House (which will receive further attention) and which will once more sit proud, a gem within a more modest urban townscape.

Left *Engraving c.1870s, showing Alloa Pottery and Bauchop's House to left of centre.* Above *Sundial, Bauchop's House.*

Alloa Pottery in the Kirkgate was founded *c.*1780 and was modestly productive until its purchase around 1856 by Joseph Bailey who *soon put new life in the business*, and was further expanded after he died in 1878 by his sons William and John. The brothers lived in neighbouring villas on Claremont: Gracedieu and Riverdieu, linked by a conservatory, designed *c.*1873 by Charles Leadbetter. The pottery produced a wide range of products but was perhaps most famous for its teapots, the finest Rockingham teapots in the world, with 100,000 always in stock at any one time. It closed in 1907 and was mostly demolished in the 1940s though a warehouse remained until *c.*1974, when thousands of priceless moulds were disposed of as it was cleared for a car park.

Broad Street Housing, 2000, Vernon Monaghan Corner of Broad Street with Stripehead marked by three-storey square bay window on impressive range of four housing blocks – an excellent piece of urban infill replacing the old Ship Inn (colour p.69). Architect's earlier Mar Street infill must have impressed, for here he provided Ochil View Housing Association with similar lead-clad dormers, traditional forms with vertically exaggerated windows and a combination of red brick and white render, similar to his Bridge Terrace housing.

Left *Broad Street Housing and rear of Careers Central Ltd.* Below *Kirkgate from Stripehead.*

8 **St John's Episcopal Church**, Broad Street, 1867–9, Sir Robert Rowand Anderson
Built on the edge of Alloa Park by the then plain Robert Anderson, styled in G G Scott inspired early geometrical gothic and dominated by impressive broach spire. Rich interior includes mosaic altarpiece by Salviati of Venice – which with the High Altar mosaic at Scott's St Paul's Episcopal Cathedral, Dundee (1853 – see *Dundee* in this series), probably provides earliest instances of mosaic work by his firm in the UK; stained glass by C E Kempe (colour p.69). In 1873 Thomas Bradshaw reckoned it to be *the most elegant place of worship in the County,* which holds true today. Ongoing restoration programme, internal alterations and repair from 1992, Colin Machin.

9 **Park School**, 1935, William Kerr
Hall, classrooms and offices accommodated in long, single-storey blocks, in roughcast brick, red tile roof and multi-paned large windows.

10 **Alloa Glass Cone**, Glasshouse Loan, *c*.1825
One of three built here and the only surviving glass cone in Scotland: a simple round cone of brick, about 60ft high, on rubble octagonal base with arched openings. Second, older cone, to south lasted until 1972.

11 Large brick-built **Bass Maltings** nearby on corner of Castle Street, 1897, are only remaining buildings of famous Younger's of Alloa. **Mackie's** bus depot, 42 Glasshouse Loan, was Charles Pearson's Craigward Cooperage, of which several buildings remain.

Top *St John's Episcopal Church*. Middle *Front elevation, Park School*. Above *Alloa Glass Cone*.

Alloa Glassworks
The United Glass factory is the oldest glassworks in Europe on its original site, founded by Lady Frances Erskine of Mar in 1750 (through the idea of her father, the exiled 6th Earl, who had been impressed with glass-making techniques he had seen in Bohemia. Craftsmen were sought from Bohemia and the works established using local raw materials: sand, lime and soda ash. Now the largest glass container factory in the United Kingdom, currently producing nearly 2½ million bottles every day.

Lime Tree Walk and Broad Street c.1910.

Forth Street (now subsumed by glassworks) and **Castle Street** formed Alloa's New Town, feued by the Erskines from 1785, though only one house built at first, with John Smith, an Alloa architect, building more houses in Castle Street, *c*.1800. Too close to industry and nothing is left.

Kilncraigs Mill, mid-19th century onwards
Precise date of the foundation of this mill not
known, though John Paton was certainly spinning
worsted yarns at Kilncraigs by 1814 when he
brought the first spinning-Jenny to the mill.

Oldest surviving part is five-storey classically
fronted mill, built before 1860. Five-storey
Burnside Mill, 1859–60, has impressive eight-
storey water tower and rare wooden cooling
tower. West Mill rebuilt, 1860, after a fire and the
Wareroom probably not long before that.

12 Company's pride is evident from **1904 office
block** by William Kerr (it brought him to Alloa)
which overlooks the kirkyard in flamboyant
Edwardian baroque, ornamented with tall arched
windows, Ionic pilasters and scrolled pediments.
Internal enrichments include fine panel work and

13 wide marble staircase. Adjacent **warehouse**
extension, 1936, also William Kerr (at the end of
his career), possibly the best building of its date
and type in Scotland; white, horizontal, well-
proportioned block enclosed within two
vertically proportioned sections indicating the
staircase and amenity rooms (colour p.70).

Left *Kilncraigs Mills, 1970.* Top *North
elevation, 1904 office block.* Middle *Office
block and 1936 warehouse.* Above *New
landscaping, across Auld Brig Road from
Kilncraigs Mill.*

Now seeking regeneration following closure of
the mill in 1999 but Clackmannanshire Council
proactive in seeking new uses for the site and has
an ambitious proposal. It is intended to retain
William Kerr's office and warehouse buildings to
provide Clackmannan College with a new town-
centre campus, and to give an imaginative new
east frontage by Law and Dunbar-Nasmith
Architects (colour p.70). New superstore will be
developed further east and, in between, a 60ft-
wide boulevard to link the town centre with Alloa
Tower. Based on the spirit of the 6th Earl's plans,
first section across Auld Brig Road completed,
2000, by Clackmannanshire Council Architects,
with Paul Hogarth Company as landscape advisor.

George Brown, 1818–80, born in Alloa,
founded the *Toronto Globe* and later
became Prime Minister of Upper Canada.

29

Top *Kilncraigs Mill and Paton School.*
Above *Alloa Candleriggs Brewery of*
George Younger c.1889, closed 1960s and
demolished soon after. Right *Maclay's*
Thistle Brewery.

Beer, which has long been brewed in Alloa, was developed commercially to profit from the population boom of the early 19th century. By 1900 Alloa contained Bass Crest, Caponcroft, Forth, Forthbank, Hutton Park, Meadow, Mills, Shore, Thistle and Townhead Breweries; and the nationally important George Younger's Candleriggs and Arrol's Alloa Breweries. As a brewing centre, the town was second only to Edinburgh, where William McEwan, 1827–1913, son of an Alloa shipowner founded his famous brewery after training in Alloa. Despite the post-war loss of overseas markets, and the general contraction of the brewing industry, Alloa retained two famous breweries until the end of the 20th century; sadly, Carlsberg Tetley's immense Alloa Brewery and Maclay's small, independent Thistle Brewery are both now closed and await redevelopment. Bass still has its maltings off Castle Street and the new modern Forth Brewery utilises an industrial estate unit at Kelliebank.

14 **Paton School**, Greenside Street, 1864, John Melvin Gothic with four-storey square tower, built for children of millworkers at bequest of Alexander Paton of Cowdenpark. Irregular gable bays added to either side, 1900, initialled *J P S & C* (John Paton, Son & Co.). Intended to form Clackmannanshire Council's new Museum and Archive Centre, by Gray Marshall Associates.
Greenside Mission Chapel, 1873, simple large chamber with three-storey gothic tower, funded by David Paton of Tillicoultry as meeting place for various missionary societies with which he was involved. From late 19th century until 1980s both buildings used as Paton's Works Canteen.

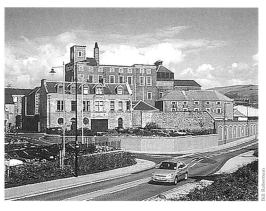

Maclay's Thistle Brewery, 1870
Maclay's, founded 1830 by James Maclay, one of the last independent Victorian breweries to function in Scotland, ceased brewing at Alloa in 1999 and has abandoned its historic and outstanding range of brick buildings, dominated by weather-vaned square tower of the brewhouse, rebuilt after a 1910 fire. Four-storey rubble and brick maltings are early 19th century (colour p.70).

15 **Office block**, facing East Vennel, 1895–6, Harbourne Maclennan, distinguished by round windows and mouldings (built before brewery acquired by Alexander Fraser of Dunfermline). All under threat but it is vital that this range of buildings is saved as a memorial to Alloa's, and indeed Scotland's, brewing heritage. Low, slated **cartshed** to Mill Road dated 1830 but probably older, and various 18th-century domestic buildings incorporated into low range to Old Bridge Street. A 1668 marriage lintel is built into the wall at junction of Old High Street and Old Bridge Street. A 1770 blacksmith's panel from a wall of Paton's, opposite, now in Clackmannanshire Council's Museum.

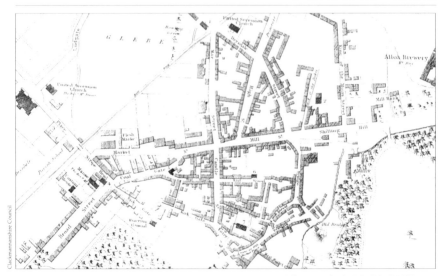

Clackmannanshire Council

TOWN CENTRE

Shillinghill forms the first section of Alloa's commercial spine, continuing into Mill Street and Bank Street to the West End. It became the principal road to Clackmannan after the original route over the Auld Brig was closed by industrialisation. Long curving street of varying character, improved now that through traffic has moved to both bypasses and by subsequent traffic management schemes, but requiring both respect and investment.

Alloa town plan by John Wood, 1825.

The name Shillinghill is derived from *sheiling* associated with hand threshing grain from the nearby corn mill, recollected by the title of one of the houses, Miller's House, 8 Shillinghill.

The Melvins were an old Alloa family, originally joiners, although other branches of the family established a foundry and a bicycle works. John Melvin Sr, 1805–84, was the first settled architect in Alloa, returning to his native town in 1826 after training in Edinburgh. He was responsible for the design (and reconstruction, continuing the family trade of joiner) of many houses, villas and churches in Alloa and district until his retiral in 1878. John Melvin Jr, 1855–1905, having trained in Edinburgh, joined and continued designing the majority of Alloa's Victorian villas – particularly in the west area of the town.

Bill Robertson

16 **Bridge Terrace**, 1996, Simister Monaghan Superb contemporary housing for Ochil View Housing Association marks the way into the town centre, vast convex façade turning the corner from Shillinghill into newly resurrected approach road to the south of the town centre, appropriately, Auld Brig Road. Its public face is like a big *liquorice allsort*: red ashlar masonry to ground floor, topped by narrow stringcourse supporting

Left and below Bridge Terrace.

Swan

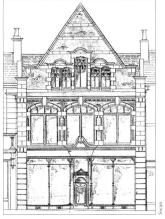

mezzanine of tiny square windows and upper floor all clad in white render. Concave elevation to rear in brick and white render fits in four storeys, with wide glazed canopy sweeping round ground floor. Car park replaces early 19th-century Alloa Meal Mill, which was on the site of an earlier mill. Stone inscribed *this mill was built 1735* (though there is a record of the mill being built in 1677) now in Clackmannanshire Council's Museum. Saltire Society Design Award, 1995.

Mill Street contains selection of two-storey plain 19th-century shops and houses, interspaced with more grandiose classical buildings. **Abbey National Building Society** (No 69) retains remnants of Art Nouveau façade of Fusco's Soda Fountain Bar, 1921, George Kerr, which served excellent coffee and ice cream until 1970s (colour p.71). It occupies half a three-storey renaissance palazzo with beautifully detailed window surrounds, topped by attic floor with gabled classical pediment. **59-63** Mill Street, *c.*1830, three-bay house, with two pilastered shopfronts and rounded slated dormers.

W E Trent's 1939 Gaumont (or La Scala) cinema has unusually flat plain geometric façade picked out in blue-and-cream tilework (now **Bingo Hall**). Trent was house architect to Gaumont cinemas in London, and the cinema was built on the site of the Savoya Café, where Charles Forte's father taught him the skills that led eventually to Trust House Forte. **Happit** (No 36), 1903, by George Kerr as the Hosiery, forms a stop to High Street. Note gothic triangular gable and windows rising above trio of renaissance round-headed windows (shopfront still a modern disaster).

Top *Mr M Fusco outside his Soda Fountain Bar, 69 Mill Street.* Middle *Elevation of Happit.* Above *59-63 Mill Street.* Right *Mill Street c.1910.*

17**41-45 Mill Street**, 1874, Adam Frame
Remarkable three-storey neo-Grecian block of Alexander 'Greek' Thomson type: first-floor

windows with finely moulded windowheads, each topped by an acanthus leaf; and space between each second-floor window decorated with dwarf pilasters over Greek key pattern.

Treetops Bar and Restaurant, 31 Mill Street, 1906, J M Dick Peddie and George Washington Browne Built as British Linen Bank and it shows: two-storey-and-attic red ashlar Jacobean facing Mill Street with pedimented doorways, balustrades above cornice at roofline, Burgh Arms shield and curvilinear gables; in short, Edwardian plush. Diagonally opposite, steep-spired turret of **26 Mill Street**, a late Victorian three-storey block, turns corner into Candleriggs, where it has attractive double shopfront. More early 19th-century two-storey shops and flats above only just hanging on, on east side of **Candleriggs**. West side and Mill Street continue with adequately scaled but not adventurous new build, 1995, Hendry and Legge. North side of Mill Street has good range of *c.*1820s' two-storey houses, now with ground-floor shops. **Coalgate**, a remnant of the Old Town street pattern, formed the road out of town via the west part of Mill Street and modern High Street (colour p.67). **Paterson's Grain Store**, 1-3 Coalgate, mid-18th-century two-storey ashlar, with scrolled skewputts, indicates where the new road abutted the original town, something the narrow angle of the older Coalgate emphasises. **Nos 5-11**, 1878, very busy mock baronial by Adam Frame with scrolls, cornices and crowsteps.

Bank Street, developed after 1810, is the continuation of Mill Street into the West End, and the scale becomes grander, more suburban and establishment Victorian. Former **Chalmers Church**, 1855–6, John J Murdoch and W H Hay, characteristically original gothic on rectangular

Top 41-45 Mill Street. Middle Treetops Bar and Restaurant. Above 5-11 Coalgate. Left Paterson's Grain Store.

Above *Former Chalmers Church in 1856.* Right *Burgh Chambers and former post office.*

Thomas Frame, 1813–75, a native of Culross, settled in Alloa in 1852 as a joiner and builder. He was joined by his son Adam, who had trained as an architect, and established Thomas Frame & Son. **Adam Frame**, 1836–1901, was one of the few provincial architects to attempt to follow Alexander Thomson's idiosyncratic Egypto-Grecian. His major works were Alloa Burgh Chambers, the former museum in Church Street and the finely detailed High Street/Mill Street corner block. The firm was continued by his son Thomas, 1878–1903, assisted from *c.*1900 by **George Twigg**, 1873–1953, who became sole principal in 1929, joined by his son Laurence, 1913–70 in 1945. The firm closed in the 1960s. **John Shaw Leishman**, 1863–1908, trained with Adam Frame and established his own firm *c.*1893 in Alloa.

Mercat Cross.

plan, the main feature the sturdy square tower, with diagonal buttressing to corners, capped by fine stone spire. Since the congregation united with St Andrew's (now North Church) in 1970, church has been abused as a nightclub – currently **Penelope's**. **Bank Bar**, *c.*1870, formerly the Crown, imposing two-storey hotel with twin projecting rectangular bays topped by classical hipped roofs, looks like a squashed country house.

19 **Burgh Chambers**, 1873–4, Adam Frame
Splendidly ornate Victorian renaissance façade, with rusticated ground floor, alternating pedimented upper floor and parapet. Nearly symmetrical, with rusticated pend arch to west bay and to the east a Corinthian-columned porch, capped with huge shield representing the burgh crest (a galley surmounted by a wreath and a trussed ram, and the motto *In the Forefront*). On first floor, bays continue with Corinthian pilasters and end with balustraded parapets. Interior reconstructed, 1907, after a fire: interesting tilework, and fine panelling and plasterwork in Council Chamber. Behind the pompous front block was a long row of primitive cells, converted to housing, and extended, by Clackmannan District Council Architects, *c.*1990, leading into Burgh Mews and Mar Street. Next door, former **post office**, a poor continuation, 1882, by Frame, now restored with good new frontage.

Mercat Cross, 1690, Tobias Bauchop
Erected as symbolic ornament by 6th Earl of Mar in the Old Market Place (now Kilncraigs Mill entrance courtyard) and re-erected in front of new Burgh Chambers in 1879. Restored mythical griffin's head sits on octagonal shaft.

Cuthbert Donaldson & Co. Solicitors
(former Commercial Bank), 18-22 Bank Street,
1848, David Rhind
Good banker's classical with fierce, quoinless
channelled stone ground floor and bracketed
cornice at roofline, by the Commercial Bank
architect. Probably the building that gave its
name to the street. Behind, more new-build
housing for Ochil View Housing Association in
two-tone brick, 1997, MBM Architects. Quality of
Art Nouveau frontage of **No 36**, 1910, George
Kerr – a simple curved transom to the window,
applied oval form, similar door treatment and
tapered columns to inside window screen –
deserves notice. Now under threat of conversion
to a flat.

Clydesdale Bank, 11 Bank Street, 1852
More opulent banker's renaissance, ashlar
stonework channelled at street level, architraved
windows above, topped by bracketed cornice.
Corner doorpiece of granite Ionic columns, full
entablature and pediment, probably added by
James Thomson. Ewing's Fountain was here until
moved to the head of Lime Tree Walk in 1870 – to
the consternation of the citizens: 400 assembled to
protest. **Housing** at Coalgate corner of Union
Street, once part of **Younger's Brewery**, has two
re-used 18th-century stones built in (one with
tailor's emblems) and huge bargeboarded upper
bow windows. Tall hipped roofed tower behind
was the **Meadow Brewery** malt kiln also
converted to housing.

36 Bank Street in 1987.

Above *Former Younger's Brewery with
Meadow Brewery malt kiln behind.* Left
Careers Central Ltd.

20 **Careers Central Ltd**, 1935–8, William Kerr
*A pleasing improvement to the architectural amenity
of one of the main entrances to Alloa* suggested the
local paper, referring to the frigid 1930s' classical
stone frontage of former gas showrooms and
offices facing Bank Street, with horizontal railings
and burgh crest. Remainder a much more

George Alexander Kerr, 1865–1927, a
native of Lockerbie and no relation to
William, came to Alloa in 1893 and
succeeded Leishman as Frame's
assistant. In 1896 he established his own
business, taking a partner, **William
McCulloch**, from 1903, the partnership
being dissolved on the latter's
emigration in 1914. Kerr produced
buildings of great quality, many with
Art Nouveau detailing, notably Grange
(now St John's Primary) School, the shop
fronts of Fusco's Cafe, 36 Bank Street
and 1 Bedford Place all surviving.

William Kerr, 1866–1940, was probably the most talented Alloa architect. He became a partner in John Melvin & Son in 1902 after having served his apprenticeship with Sir John James Burnet under Alexander MacGibbon (1885–90), and then being principal assistant to Thomas Graham Abercrombie of Paisley (1890–1902). A native of Houston, Renfrewshire, he continued to live there and commuted to Alloa by train, reputedly sketching out schemes on his stiff white cuffs during the journey. Although most of Kerr's early works in Alloa, like Paton's office block and the Liberal Club, both 1904, are strictly classical, from his arrival he was producing subtle undecorated buildings using powerful roof forms and tall Lutyenesque bay windows. These include Sauchie Public Hall, Paton's Sports Pavilion and the Cochrane Hall in Alva. In the l930s he produced buildings comparable to those of any of the young avant-garde architects. In 1912, he took a partner, **John Gray**, to whom a share of the credit for buildings attributed to Kerr after this date must be given. Kerr died in 1940 and in 1946, a few months before John Gray's death, Gordon Biggar became a partner. The firm was dissolved in 1985 on the latter's retiral.

Right War Memorial with Weir Pumps Social and Recreation Club behind (see p.43). Below 15 Mar Street c.1905.

adventurous composition in cream-painted harling punctured by long strip windows, successfully transformed into housing. Elevation to Coalgate previously contained flat-roofed tiny shops, flanked by two huge cinemaesque ovoid towers, massing to central tower.

21 **War Memorial**, Bank Street, 1923–4, Sir Robert Lorimer
Fine bronze sculpted by C d'O Pilkington Jackson, *A female figure with mural crown and shield, symbolising the Thought of Alloa, following her sons in battle. The shield bears the town's arms.* (*Alloa Advertiser*, 1924). She is surrounded by soldiers cutting barbed wire and is set in a landscaped stage flanked by a curved screen wall of stone.

Mar Street (originally Cowie's Loan) was one of the streets laid out in the late 18th-century improvements, when additional streets were feued by the Erskines. Former **Hope Bakery** (No 1) has pilastered shopfront *c.*1830. Rear shop has two historic ovens: the 1810 one was the oldest continuously working commercial oven in Scotland until the bakery's closure in 2000, the newer oven dates from 1840.

22 **15 Mar Street**, 1904, William Kerr
Former Liberal Club in symmetrical Jacobean with fine Doric-columned door. First-floor club rooms identified by tall mullioned oriel bays, whereas former billiard rooms above have sculpted dormer windows behind Art Nouveau balustrading, some with stained glass by Oscar Paterson (colour p.72). Interiors have excellent woodwork and many original features. Part of ground floor was retained by Kerr's firm, John Melvin and Son, until 1985, as its office with

original screens, benches and other joinery work; the rooms survive though the specific architects' furniture has gone. Now various offices.

Alloa Job Centre.

23 **Alloa Job Centre**, 1932, William Kerr
Converted from Alloa Co-operative Society's headquarters and for a long time the district library, façade is 1930s' classical in sandstone. Fluted pilasters flank the door with suitable date stones and emblems above.

19 Mar Street, *c*.1825–30
Classical house of dressed stone, entered through projecting pedimented central bay, between Ionic columns and under a fanlight, operating as offices and the Resource Centre. Behind is William Kerr and John Gray's 1936–8 YMCA hall, in the pattern of large multi-paned windows, harled brickwork and low parapet walls which Kerr developed for other local halls and schools; now re-used as **Alloa Children's Centre** and **CliCk** (Community Learning in Clackmannanshire), and leading into Burgh Mews (see Bank Street, p.34) and 1988 housing by Bracewell Stirling Architects. **Bank of Scotland**, 21 Mar Street, 1832, Robert Black, designed as a bank, which may explain the more stolid Doric order for the columns. Major extension to north side, 1991, Davis Duncan Partnership, neatly tucked out of sight.

St Mungo's RC Church and **Presbytery**, 1960–1, William W Friskin
Fronted by massive five-light gable, this huge church is traditional in form, yet constructed of brown brick, with vertical louvred slits to the square belfry. Inside is wide, white and bright, with narrow aisles supported on tall octagonal columns. Lady Chapel has three contemporary

Below *Side elevation, Alloa Job Centre.* Middle *Bank of Scotland.* Bottom *St Mungo's RC Church and Presbytery.*

20 Mar Street and former Alloa Advertiser.

small stained-glass windows by Sadie McLellan representing her first public commission in the *Dalles de Verre* medium. Like the church, adjacent brick presbytery also has stone embellishments, but style more akin to early 1900s' villas by John Melvin on Claremont, with semicircular plan stairtower and hipped slated roofs.

Former Alloa Advertiser, 1952, Arthur Bracewell A 1950s' façade in original condition, stonework to ground floor elaborately curved with three doors and two windows. Small balcony in wrought iron sits above central door. **20 Mar Street**, 1992, Simister Monaghan, excellent infill for Ochil View Housing Association, providing six flats for young single persons within symmetrical three-bay block topped by lead-clad dormers – a contemporary take on George Kerr's 'eyebrow' motif.

24 **Sheriff Court House**, 1863–4, Brown and Wardrop Built as County and Police Buildings to replace Ochil House, in imposing late French Gothic, with crowstepped gablets and tall slender windows in ones, twos and threes. Three-storey rectangular tower with high French roof marks Drysdale Street corner. Matching extension, 1910, and Police Offices, 1938 (now Citizens' Advice Bureau), added by William Kerr.

Sheriff Court House.

25 **Ochil House**, mid-18th century
Originally the Plough Inn, converted in 1820 into a Tontine Hotel; from 1844–63 County Offices and Court; in 1882 headquarters for volunteer army groups; in 1970s the social work department; and from 1993, restored as offices by Colin Machin and now headquarters of Ochil View Housing Association (with the loss of two cells at lower ground-floor level, survivors of its use as a court). Fairly expansive, two storey, entered through projecting pedimented bay: note carving of plough in pediment. **Earl of Mar Court**, 1993–4, Bracewell Stirling Architects, opposite Town Hall, provides Ochil View Housing Association with plain but traditionally proportioned, two-storey staggered-plan terraces of housing for the elderly, on site of former drill hall and rifle range.

26 **Mar Place House**, early 19th century
Set in delightful garden, simple Georgian ashlar house, with Ionic-columned door and single-storey wings; provides attractive dentists' surgery.

Top *Ochil House*. Middle *Earl of Mar Court and Wagon Road*. Above *Mar Place House*. Left *Moncrieff United Free Church*.

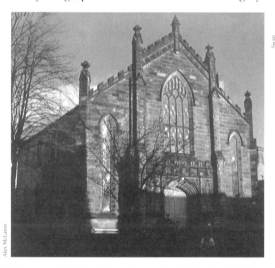

27 **Moncrieff United Free Church**, 1850, John Melvin
On site of old Secession Church, it is the gable that matters: huge with crenellated parapet and pinnacle buttresses, enfolding large traceried window flanked by narrow lancet windows. Original features inside include box pews, horseshoe gallery and 1884 organ by Lewis & Co. in original condition and in use. Round the entrance are fine cast-iron balustraded steps. **Moncrieff House**, former manse, *c*.1834, solid classical with Doric door and hipped roof.

Tontine Hotel
A tontine is a business arrangement invented by the Neopolitan Lorenzo Tonti, where the investment increases as other subscribers die. A number of tontine hotels were established in the early 19th century, such as at Glasgow (famously on Trongate), Ayr, Peebles and Greenock (see *Central Glasgow, Ayrshire & Arran, Borders & Berwick* and *The South Clyde Estuary* in this series).

70 Drysdale Street.

70 Drysdale Street (former County Offices), 1926, William Kerr
Imposing Jacobean, symmetrical frontage reminiscent of much earlier Liberal Club, Mar Street, with heavy mullioned leaded windows. Above the simple door is county motto *Look About Ye.*

28 **Former Townhead Institute**, Drysdale Street, 1914–15, William Kerr
Arts & Crafts, in white harled brick under immense swept roof; small horizontal windows with louvred shutters, high underneath the eaves. Large openings to Drysdale Street have plain stone mullions and date stones; upper windows open to wrought-iron balustraded balcony. Built as Temperance YMCA clubrooms (on site of popular Prince of Wales hostelry) by paternalistic Forrester-Paton family, later the Townhead Tearooms. Now flatted with shops and café.

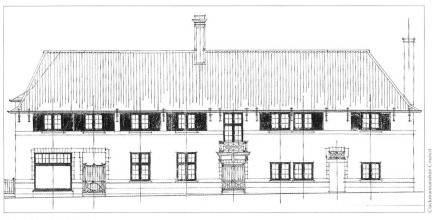

Former Townhead Institute.

High Street
Formerly High Coalgate; now, with Mill Street, one of Alloa's principal commercial streets. West

High Street, c.1930s–40s.

side rebuilt, 1870s. **Nos 8-16** form interesting symmetrical range, centred gable with rounded dormer wings, sadly out of scale with Adam Frame's neo-Greek building on corner of Mill Street. Some original shopfronts survive, suggestive of the quality to which others could be restored.

East side escaped Victorian but not modern development; David MacGibbon's 1861 Scots Baronial **National Bank** at the corner of Mill Street a particular loss. **Royal Bank of Scotland**, 1909, J M Dick Peddie, English baroque palace, with grand fluted Corinthian pilasters supporting elaborate sculptured central pediment with the bank's arms.

Primrose Street

Once a residential street leading to the little valley of the Fairy Burn (on which first the railway station then the leisure centre was built), now a mixture of shopfronts of different eras. **The Co-op** is everywhere in this part of Alloa; main three-storey block, 1935, has fabulous moderne detailing by SCWS Architecture Department, rebuilt after 1957 fire, with earlier (1887, Adam Frame) and more recent buildings behind. **Drysdale Street Co-operative**, 1895, Adam Frame and 1862 High Street Co-op Pharmacy building with 1912 clock.

Station Hotel (once Victoria Hotel), dated 1880, continues as public house with flats above (Primrose Court), a rich building with ornate moulded doorway, carved stone details and corner bay windows, and rabble of run-down extensions backing onto Wagon Road. **Factory Direct**, Nos 10-12, has Corinthian-columned first floor, and tiny **Primrose Cottage**, possibly John Melvin, originally Townhead or United Presbyterian School, run by the Moncrieff Church, incongruously set back from street behind its garden.

41

Speirs Centre, former Alloa Public Baths:
Top *Turkish Bath;* Right *Primrose Place and Primrose Street elevations;* Above *Banister.*

30 **Speirs Centre**, 1895–8, Burnet, Son and Campbell
Splendidly powerful Scots Renaissance former
Public Baths and Gymnasium by distinguished
Glasgow architects; elevation to Primrose Place of
particular quality. Partly modernised, but retains
tilework, balustrading and sculpture of a strong
Moorish and Oriental character. Baths hall (now
floored over as sports hall) not much altered from
the Victorian period, when there were cubicles
round the walls, potted palms, and trapezes
swinging from the roof (see p.5). Spectacular tiled
Turkish baths suite is lost. Baths presented to the
town by John Thomson-Paton of Norwood and
Kilncraigs Mill who also sponsored the Town
Hall. It should be refurbished for its original
purpose; currently houses Clackmannanshire
Council's Museum and Heritage Service, pending
relocation (colour p.71).

Alloa Glebe
The glebe, serving the former manse at the head
of Broad Street, stretched northwards from
Bedford Place to Marshill. Developed, 1870s, to
form Ludgate (Street), Coningsby Place, Glebe
Terrace and Church Street: rows of Victorian
villas many by Adam Frame. Collectively
interesting for variety of large and small, single,
double and flatted villas, with classical and Scots
31 Baronial features, **Birkendale**, 2-4 Coningsby
Place, dated 1872, is notable: double villa by
Adam Frame, western half for himself. **Oakleigh**,
2 Glebe Terrace, dated 1890. Junction of Glebe
Terrace and Coningsby Place forms impressive
streetscape with vast **West End Park** in the

Glebe Terrace.

distance, opened 1878, bought by the burgh from the Earl of Mar and Kellie, entered through impressive stone gateway from Grange Road.

32 **Weir Pumps Social and Recreation Club**, Church Street, 1873, Adam Frame
Built as Museum Hall for Alloa Society of Natural Science and Archaeology, later public library, behind frigidly symmetrical façade composed round classical pediment propped up on four squat columns of Alexander 'Greek' Thomson derivation.

Bedford Place and **Grange Road** formed a principal route west to Stirling, through spacious Regency and Victorian suburbs. **1 Bedford Place**, 1910, built as garage and cycle shop for J B Whyte by George Kerr, retains curved Art Nouveau windows, though façade altered for SMS Motor Accessory Store. **Royal Oak Hotel**, No 7, 1820s, cream-painted ashlar, with unusual pilastered ends to the façade.

33 **West Church**, 1864, Peddie and Kinnear
On site of Associate Burgher Church. Gothic, with rectangular plan and tall campanile at south-west corner, given Scots Gothic transepts and sanctuary in Oregon pine and marble, 1902, by Sydney Mitchell and Wilson. Three stained-glass windows by C E Kempe and 1903 organ – still in use – by Lewis & Co. **Church Hall**, 1891, Adam Frame. Across **Bedford Place**, former

34 **Burgh School**, 1875, John Melvin, elaborate Scots Baronial: circular entrance tower with conical roof and crowstepped gable with mullioned triple window, extended 1910, George Kerr.

Top *Weir Pumps Social and Recreation Club*. Middle *1 Bedford Place c.1920.* Above *West Church.*

Bedford Place showing the former Burgh School and St Mungo's Parish Church: little has changed.

St Mungo's Parish Church.

35 **St Mungo's Parish Church**, 1817–19,
James Gillespie Graham
Unusually delicate and picturesque for a
Gillespie Graham unscholarly revival church.
Usual symmetry in plan, but greater felicity than
normal in lacy perpendicular gothic; a 207ft-high
spire with flying buttresses, rising from the tower
to the centre of the south frontage. Each corner of
church graced with low square tower with
crenellated parapet. Spire is precursor of Gillespie
Graham's larger version at Montrose. Interior and
additions at gables by Leslie Grahame
MacDougall in Lorimer-derived gothic. William
Kerr added classical **Church Hall**, 1926
(converted to eight flats, with new housing
behind, for Ochil View Housing Association,
1997, MBM Architects, and opened by this
author). Church needs community facilities and
has an exciting scheme in mind for an elliptical
hall to be created within its east end, with
balcony above, by Page and Park Architects,
modelled on successful examples in Glasgow.

Nos 9, **10**, **12**, **13** and **16 Bedford Place** all date
from about the year of Waterloo, classical villas in
their own grounds overlooking the Forth, using
standard components of classical architecture –
pilasters, columns, fanlights, architraves – to
achieve individuality.

Fentoun House.

    Fentoun House, 11 Bedford Place, *c*.1840, cut-
stone classical, with fine moulded windows,
architraves, pediments and a pilastered door:
substantial stable block to rear. It was home to
James Moir, factor to the Earls of Mar,

Above and right *Bedford Court.*

Abercrombys of Tullibody, Johnstones of Alva
36 and agent of the Commercial Bank. **Bedford
House**, 13 Bedford Place, *c*.1855, of similar
proportions, but more ornate. Behind is **Bedford
Court**, 1985, Wheeler and Sproson, Saltire Society
award-winning scheme of sheltered housing.
Two-storey houses fairly plain but staggered rows
of single-storey cottages and communal facilities

Opposite from top *Lylestone House:
garden front; stair mural; Ionic capital;
Old Rectory.*

44

Robert Bald, 1775–1861, son of the superintendent of the Alloa coal works, is remembered as the *enlightened mining engineer* of the Earls of Mar, who were extracting coal from Sauchie until the Alloa Coal Company was formed in 1844. Although, in 1832, he attributed miners' deaths from cholera to the *immoderate drinking of whisky*, he was a firm supporter of the Earl of Shaftesbury's Mines and Collieries Bill (1842) abolishing apprenticeship in mines and excluding women and boys from working underground. Bald wrote: *A stout woman carried in general from a hundredweight to two hundredweight and in a trial of strength three hundredweight imperial … It was not uncommon for the women ascending the stairs from the pit bottom to the surface to weep most bitterly from the severity of the labour.* One woman complained to him: *Oh sir, this is some work. I wish to God that the first woman who tried to bear coals had broken her back and none would have tried again.* Just prior to his death in 1861, Bald was recognised as having *rendered important services … throughout Europe, as a mining engineer* and had done much *to ameliorate the condition of the mining population.* His brother **Alexander Bald**, 1783–1859, who ran the timber-yard and brick and tile works at Craigward, wrote a then indispensable book for Scottish tenant farmers, *The Corn Dealers Assistant*, and was a patron and friend to many literary figures, being among the first to acknowledge James Hogg, the Ettrick Shepherd.

forming courtyards behind still impress.
8 Bedford Place, *c*.1815, set in walled garden, entered through rusticated gatepiers and Doric-columned doorway, faces south, originally overlooking the Forth; note Venetian window.

37 **Lylestone House**, 10 Bedford Place, 1815, fine, south-facing, with elaborate windows on both façades, an Ionic-columned porch facing the street, a Doric one the garden. Circular, domed stair decorated with unusual mural painting of Edinburgh from Fife, complete with steamboats. House was home of the noted mining engineer, Robert Bald. **Westray**, 1814–15, next door, contemporary, smaller and somewhat more delicate.

Grange Road continues Bedford Place and **Nos 1 & 2** date from *c*.1830. Solid Doric doorpieces, ashlar stonework channelled at ground level and single-storey wings to each side. **3 Grange Road**, 1838, fine house with original window bars and

38 pilastered doorpiece. **Old Rectory**, *c*.1840, distinguished classical house, with Doric-columned door, cornice, architraved windows, and well-proportioned side wings. Octagonal chimneypots worth a glance.

From top *29-31 Grange Road; 40 Grange Road; ABC Nursery; 38-50 Grant Street.*

St John's Primary School: Right *Central hall;* Below *Tiled dado.*

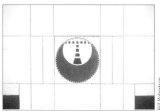

13 Grange Road, 1840s, has ornamental pedestal at the centre, flanked by two bay windows; entrance porch in a wing to the east. Note flower carving on window lintels of **29-31 Grange Road**, 1870s, comparable to Adam Frame's Church Street Museum, implying possibly the same hand. **35-39 Grange Road**, 1880s, block of three plain houses unified by lovely wrought-iron door pediments. **40 Grange Road**, another 1830s' villa, has its back to the main road and another fine Doric-columned door.

39 **ABC Nursery**, Grant Street, 1902, William Kerr Converted from St John's Primary School, this red brick courtyard is in what became Kerr's usual style with large multi-paned windows, green slate roof and belfry, fronted by new conservatory, 40 1994. **38-50 Grant Street**, rare 1903 terrace of workers' houses by Sir John Burnet in Arts & Crafts: square brick columns, wooden porch lintels and long rows of dormers, all now missing their multi-pane windows and original doors. Built for T E Lander of the British Electric Plant (later Harland Engineering, now Weir Pumps) which started manufacturing switch gear, motors and generators in Alloa in 1900, and likely needed accommodation to attract specialist workers.

41 **St John's Primary School** (former Grange School), Grange Road, 1908, George Kerr
Art Nouveau in red sandstone, symmetrical block with two huge gabled bays, with Art Nouveau lettering at first-floor level. Quality is comparable with Mackintosh's Glasgow or W G Lamond's Dundee schools and is very like James Miller's Lintwhite School, Bridge of Weir (see *Central Glasgow*, *Dundee* and *The South Clyde Estuary* in this series). Well-preserved interior, with rooms planned round galleried central hall, and Kerr expressed his Christian ideals with improving inscriptions such as *Study to show thyself approved unto God*, and tiled dado of Christian symbols round the hall. Bicycle sheds now the school's nursery.

Left *St John's Primary School*. Above *1910 cottage by William Kerr now marooned between the railway line and Stirling Road*. Below *Cowdenpark*. Middle *Original drawing of Cowdenpark*. Bottom *Norwood (demolished)*.

42 **Cowdenpark**, Stirling Road, 1850, John Melvin
Tudor-Jacobean mansion for Alexander Paton of Kilncraigs Mill, with harled gabled frontage, with strong horizontal stringcourses exaggerated into architraves round window heads. Being converted back from social work offices to house – and apartments – once more. Nearby **lodge**, and the
43 lodge at Claremont, belonged to John Thomson-Paton's splendid mansion, **Norwood**, 1874, John Melvin, demolished (colour p.72).

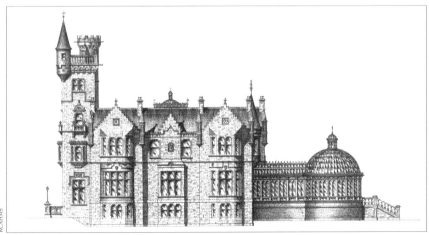

Paton is a name long associated with the district. James Paton of Balliliesk, Muckhart, was ordained as Bishop of Dunkeld in 1572, later to be dismissed for having *no function or charge in the Reformed Kirk.* In 1702 a John Paton of Cowden, near Muckhart, died. About 1760 James, 1731–84, and Andrew Paton, 1736–1822, left Muckhart to become weavers and dyers in Alloa. James' son, John Paton, 1768–1848, established the successful Kilncraigs spinning mill made famous by his descendants. His elder sons James, 1797–1882, and David, d.1891, founded their own textile mill at Tillicoultry long continued by James' family. Kilncraigs passed to John Paton's daughters, for his third son Alexander (of Cowdenpark) died without a successor in 1860. John Thomson-Paton, 1831–1910, of Norwood, donor of the town hall and public baths, and David Paton Thomson, 1843–1917, of Greenfield House were sons of the eldest daughter. Mary, 1813–81; Janet, 1798–1880, the youngest Paton daughter, founded the Forrester-Paton family, exponent of the Temperance Movement, and the great patrons of Alloa, latterly of Inglewood and The Gean. Paton's combined with Baldwins of Halifax in 1920 and with Coats of Paisley, finally becoming Coats Viyella in 1986.

Right *Arnsbrae House.* Below *Stable block, Arnsbrae House.*

Alex McLaren

Bill Robertson

Above *Tilework, Alloa Town Hall.*
Right *Alloa Town Hall.*

Over the railway a new bridge leads to Alloa's two new business parks. **Smart Village Business Campus**, 2001, Bradford Robertson, and **Pavilions Business Park**, 2001, ADF Partnership. Both have potential for more challenging buildings.

Arnsbrae House, Stirling Road, 1885, Alfred Waterhouse, extended by Paul Waterhouse
Hiding behind trees, red rubble, gabled mansion of the Younger family has gothic doorway, arched loggia and an elegant terrace. The 1885 **stable block** has been converted to housing. T-plan **lodge** with half-timbered gables and decorative ridges.

Clackmannanshire Council

Marshill
Alloa Town Hall, 1888, Alfred and Paul Waterhouse
Its huge entrance gable, with large arched doorpiece and curvilinear gable, dominates the ring road. Donated by John Thomson-Paton of Norwood, whose sculpted bust sits in the entrance hall, the hall has many fine architectural details, including Ionic pilasters, chimney and marvellously tiled staircase. It included Alloa's first public library whose running costs the townspeople had to contribute towards in their rates. In two-storey roofspace were well-lit science rooms and art studios for the town's benefit. Upgraded early 1990s.

Andrew Millar

44 **Marshill House** and **6 Marshill**, two more of
45 Alloa's early 19th-century classical villas, with
good columned porches and fine marble,
plasterwork, and fireplaces inside.

Claremont Business Centre, Ludgate, 1844,
probably John Melvin
The centre re-uses rather plain former Alloa
Academy Infant School, later the academy's
Technical School. Fronting it on Ludgate, with
simple low ashlar stone frontage to Marshill
corner, is *new workshop* of 1900, R A Bryden, and
behind infant school are workrooms, 1929,
William Kerr, simple harled block with multi-
pane windows. Centre is only remnant of original
school complex: whole school latterly served as St
Mungo's RC School before closing, main
academy of 1824–6 long demolished and its site
further west, originally separated by the railway,
now occupied by tall rendered housing blocks
which fit well into the townscape. Tall yellow
brick housing blocks on opposite corner, 2000,
Inglis and Carr.

46 **South African War Memorial**, 1904,
Robert Lorimer
Quietly forgotten within verdant shrubberies of
peaceful memorial garden, relocated monument
sculpted to Lorimer's design by W B Birnie
Rhind: a Highlander, with hand on revolver,
standing over a wounded colleague. Over-
zealous stone cleaning has inexcusably resulted
in loss of detail.

Kellie Place has a number of late Victorian Scots
villas by John Melvin. **Claremont Lodge Hotel**
(formerly the Endrick) and its neighbouring twin,
*c.*1880, large detached villas with Franco-Gothic
towers echoing County Buildings.

Claremont was the old road from Alloa to Stirling,
a quiet rural road, until it was developed for large
villas after railway bridge built at Marshill, 1851.
Modest villas on north side, most from the turn of
the century. George Kerr intended **No 38**, 1898,
half of a double villa, to be his own home, but was
47 unable to move owing to illness. **No 30**, *c.*1900,
probably Adam Frame, is a modest villa, its
Egyptian door columns again showing influence
of Alexander 'Greek' Thomson.
  Houses on south side are much grander.
Claremont Grove (No 21), vast Georgianised
house with 1913 west wing by William Kerr.
No 31, 1902, William McCulloch (later George

Top *Marshill House*. Middle *Claremont
Business Centre*. Above *South African
War Memorial*.

30 Claremont.

Kerr's partner), plain Victorian corner mansion, more typical of Glasgow dormitory towns.

48 **Struan House** (No 33), 1905, William Kerr, white harled L-plan, not unlike contemporary houses by Charles Rennie Mackintosh, now school for autistic children with remarkable specialist playroom and splash-pool pavilion extension, 1990, Aitken and Turnbull. **Craigmyle**, 1902, John Melvin, has very steep hipped roof, canted bay windows to south and three-storey round tower. Unmistakable hand of William Kerr in detailing of columned porch.

Craig-na-Aird (No 37), 1902, and **Claremont**
49 **House** (No 39), 1901, both by Melvin, latter very similar to Craigmyle, but on larger scale. Built as parish manse and was home to the late Earl of Mar and Kellie. Ornamental features include rainwater heads in the form of fish. New manse built at foot of extensive garden *c*.1950.

Claremont has expanded westwards along both sides of the ridge, with 1930s' bungalows, more recent speculative housing estates and the vast **Alloa Academy** complex, 1957 onwards, County Architect, with two-tone brick refronting, 1987–9, Central Region Architects. Steeply pitched tiled roofs have double tiers of dormers; there are planted walls, pavilion blocks and clocktower dated 1989.

Right *Struan House*. From top *Struan House; Craigmyle; Claremont House: north front; south front.*

Alloa Academy.

50

Top and above *The Gean*.

Below *Bathroom, The Gean*.
Bottom *Gean Lodge*.

The Gean, Tullibody Road, 1912, William Kerr
One of Kerr's finest buildings, set in vast grounds,
The Gean is a large English-style mansion house
clearly influenced by Sir Edwin Lutyens.
Mullioned and transomed windows, high, red-tile
roof with tiny dormer windows, large gables and
chimneys, tower and classical porch, matched by
equal splendour inside: carved panelling,
balustrading and plasterwork. Built for Alexander
Forrester-Paton as a wedding present from his
parents. Sumptuously restored from 1990,
Simpson and Brown Architects, as country-house
hotel; completed 2000 by Clackmannanshire
Enterprise as conference centre (colour p.71).
Behind the walled garden, **Orchard Lodge**
bedroom pavilion, 2000–1, John Nicol Jarvie, in
complementary contemporary manner (colour
p.71). **Gean Lodge** (South Lodge), Claremont and
Arnsgrove, 1912, William Kerr, miniature Arts &
Crafts country house, with half-timber detailing
and sweeping tiled roofs. **North Lodge**, off
Tullibody Road, a small pavilion.

Dunmar House Hotel, Dunmar Drive, *c*.1905,
probably William Kerr
Delightful large asymmetrical two-storey villa,
similar to Kerr's Kellyside (see p.128): Anglicised
Arts & Crafts half timbering and white plaster
above stone base, complex gabled roofs, big
chimneys and multi-pane glazing (colour p.72).
Large new function suite replicates the style.

Inglewood, Tullibody Road, 1900,
A G Sydney Mitchell and Wilson
Huge symmetrical Jacobean house for Alexander
Forrester-Paton. South frontage has two-storey
bay windows with veranda, rising to huge
curved and triangular shaped gables. Four-storey

Top *Inglewood*. Above *Drawing Room, Inglewood, c.1900*. Right *Ground-floor plan of Inglewood, A G Sydney Mitchell and Wilson*.

tower rises to south east and, to north, a Doric-columned porch. Rich plasterwork and panelling inside, with glasswork by Oscar Paterson (see p.5). Restored by Clackmannanshire Enterprise as business centre. **East Lodge** at risk – derelict for 25 years – and **Coach House** re-used by Alman Dramatic Club (one of Scotland's oldest) as the Coach House Theatre. Both have similar features to the main house. **West Lodge** smaller, half timbered to the road, with canted bay to the drive. Gateway (blocked) of original main drive has half-rusticated piers, arched footgates and urn finials.

To rear of main house, at edge of woodland, the business centre has been complemented by **Forrester Lodge**, 2000, new offices by McEachern MacDuff Architects in traditional L-plan form, with steep gabled roofs and re-entrant chimney, but using blockwork and with more contemporary vertical glazing, glass-roofed entrance and two-storey *inglenook* bay window in the gable.

Below *Coach House, Inglewood*. Bottom *Forrester Lodge*.

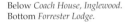

50 **Former Paton and Baldwin's Sports Pavilion**, Tullibody Road, 1926, William Kerr
Wide overhanging, red-tiled roof, with hipped roof wings to either side, shelters façades of white-painted, harled brickwork, punctured by horizontal windows along roofline and low

glazed veranda between the wings. To either side of wings are bell-roofed octagonal towers, and in centre of main roof ridge is an imposing clock turret. Still serves former employees as bowling pavilion, its north playing fields subsumed by housing. **96-98 Tullibody Road**, 1908, William Kerr, harled brick double villa with tall chimneystacks, half-timber detailing and veranda porches – some regrettable modern windows.

51 **Alloa North Church**, Ludgate, 1882,
Adam Frame
Built as St Andrew's Parish Church, tall and gothic, on prominent gushet site of Ludgate, or Round Toll. Contemporaries admired *the massive appearance emphasised by the bold proportions of the buttresses and deep splays on the window jambs and the high pitch of the roof.* **Alloa Baptist Church**, opposite, simple 1881 rectangle in *modified gothic style* by James Mitchell.

52 **Clackmannanshire Council Headquarters**, Greenfield, 1892–4, A G Sydney Mitchell and Wilson
Set in flat, well-wooded parkland, Greenfield is a good example of the red sandstone aspirations of a rich merchant, who went to Edinburgh for the most fashionable architects of the day. David Paton Thomson, grandson of John Paton of Kilncraigs, took down previous house and built a great towered confection complete with look-out tower, two-storey bay windows and tall chimneys. Reconstructed and extended after a 1914 fire, many original fittings remain including fine wood panelling and plasterwork, particularly in the Council Chamber. Bought by the Town

Top Former Paton and Baldwin's Sports Pavilion c.1930. Middle 96-98 Tullibody Road. Above Alloa North Church c.1900.

Clackmannanshire Council Headquarters, Greenfield, drawn by Alex Brown.

Parkway Court.

Council in 1952, now principal offices of Clackmannanshire Council, its grounds a public park. Extended sympathetically to the rear, 1986, Clackmannan District Council Architects. Civic Trust Commendation, 1987.

At the corner of Parkway, good new infill 53 housing, **Parkway Court**, 1990, Campbell and Arnott for Hanover Housing Association, in two-tone brick with heavy window margins, balcony mosaics at street corner and giant sundial facing the leisure centre reading *moved by the light*.

Alloa Co-operative Society Bowling Club Pavilion and Sunnyside Primary School c.1930.

Below *Clackmannan County Hospital.*
Bottom *Sunnyside Primary School.*

54 **Alloa Co-operative Society Bowling Club Pavilion**, Sunnyside Road, 1925, George Kerr
A handsome cream coloured Pavilion in the Scots domestic style, it faces west, with little hipped roof towers at the corners, veranda, balcony and elliptical roof lights to upper hall. In need of restoration – especially the column mosaics. Nearby new housing for Ochil View Housing Association, 1995, Bracewell Stirling Architects, in polychromatic brick and render.

55 **Clackmannan County Hospital**, Ashley Terrace, 1897–9, R A Bryden
Cottage hospital sponsored by Miss C Forrester-Paton, fronting original Alloa Hospital, built 1868 (the year cutlasses were first issued to the burgh police force).

56 **Sunnyside Primary School**, Erskine Street, 1892, John Bennie Wilson
Imposing symmetrical red and grey stone board school, of classrooms round tiled hall and gallery above. Inscribed pediments and neat twin belfries. Segregation of pupils by sex was the priority in its planning. Large two-storey extension to east, 1998, Clackmannanshire

Council Architects, simple rectangular block in red stone over cream render, with references to main block in its window detailing.

Clackmannan Road is the main thoroughfare
57 heading east from Alloa Town Centre. **Park Villas** built from 1872 by local builders (Gloag) and joiners (Ferguson), soon followed by Park Place. Opposite, with slight classical embellishments, is former Alloa House lodge, 1860s, probably John Melvin. Lone Scots pseudo doocot gatepost supposedly brought from Kellie Castle (see *The Kingdom of Fife* in this series) when the titles Earl of Mar and Kellie were first united. George Angus' gothic **St John the Evangelist's Episcopal Church**, 1839–40, at west end, taken over as St Mungo's RC Chapel in 1869 when the Episcopalians moved to Broad Street; finally demolished, 1969, its last use a council store, following move to Mar Street in 1961.

Hawkhill
58 Local authority housing on south side dates from 1948; side porches have modernist aspirations. Little scheme of attractive cottage housing, 1986, Clackmannan District Council Architects, hidden behind earlier scheme.

Cross Slab, Hawkhill
Early Christian standing stone, with rough incised cross to either side, lies south of the road, between Alloa and Clackmannan.

Whins Road
59 **Alloa Brewery**, established on its site, 1810, but present complex – closed 1997 and now redundant – mostly 1950s (redeveloped for Ind Coope), offers an opportunity for appropriate re-use. Brewery car park was the site of Thomson Brothers' **Springfield Mill**, a spinning and carding factory founded 1844, burnt *c*.1901. **Hutton Park**, 1945, Burgh Architect, included 80 non-traditional houses and 20 Swedish timber houses, in post-war effort to construct quick new homes. A few timber houses remain, in standard blocks of four and two, tucked away in Wallace Street and Sutherland Avenue.
60   **Carsebridge Distillery**, founded 1799 by John Bald, still provides distillery warehousing, but **Cooperage Way**, 2001, Bracewell Stirling Architects, now occupies distillery site and provides Clackmannanshire Enterprise with simple three-storey office buildings and single-storey flexible business units. **Carsebridge House**, sturdy, Victorianised, late 18th-century

Below *Alloa Brewery*. Middle *Waterwheel, c.1920, which pumped the mine shaft to the north of Carsebridge Distillery*. Bottom *Carsebridge House*.

Swan

Clackmannanshire Council

Bill Robertson

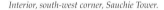

The Napoleon Pillar (*above*) is a Doric column dating from the Roman occupation of Egypt. Its inscription reads: *This Pillar was conquest of Napoleon at Grand Cairo in Egypt in the year 1798 and having been captured by the Allies en route to France was sent by them to Florence where it was bought by my Father C E DEDE and forwarded to Altona Schleswig Holstein by Fraulein DEDE, Altona den 14 ten August 1852. Above Pillar presented to J B Harvey by Mrs Dede.*

Interior, south-west corner, Sauchie Tower.

dwelling, with walled garden containing Doric **column** looted in Egypt by Napoleon. **Gaberston**, another Victorian mill, produced tartan shawls, plaids and handkerchiefs for David Lambert from 1837, later subsumed into Paton's. Gaberston Farm and Gaberston House are reminders that this was once a rural area.

Alloa Business Centre, once National Coal Board and then council premises and known as the Whins. Now provides Clackmannanshire Enterprise with various rather utilitarian multi-occupation offices and business units, with new build and extensions, 1995–9, Bracewell Stirling Architects, including **Carsebridge Court**, 1996, across main road.

SAUCHIE

Old Sauchie (place of the willows) grew up round the old Tower on the northern slopes of the Devon valley. But, as the later Sauchie landlords – Schaws and Cathcarts – prospered as mine owners, their estate workers became miners and the settlement moved south to the mines leaving the Tower almost isolated. When the Schaw family moved to Schawpark, the mining village near them became Newtonschaw. The Earl of Mar's miners' cottages at Holton Square was the first of many colliery rows in the area, and by mid-19th century – with the collected mining villages becoming *New Sauchie* – almost a suburb of Alloa.

Sauchie Tower, *c.*1430
On fine site with spectacular views north over the Devon to the Ochils, Sauchie owes its survival to fashion: the fashion that led the Schaws to abandon the Tower and its fine courtyard buildings for their splendid new seat of Schawpark near Fishcross, *c.*1700.

Begun by Sir James Schaw, whose family had come from Greenock 100 years earlier to marry the daughter of Henri de Annand of Sauchie, the Tower is built of beautifully squared blocks of pink sandstone (unusual sign of quality shared with Clackmannan) and stands to four storeys with caphouse. Parapet walk with roundels in the corners corbelled out on machicolations for the deterrence of strangers below. As usual, principal internal room on first floor, with bedrooms above; some rooms within wall thickness. Vaulted ground-floor cellar has unusual *entresol* fitted in beneath the vault, as later private room. Hall above contains grand fireplace with finely sculpted jambs, windows

Sauchie Tower.

with stone benches and stone wash basin with carved gothic head.

Tower currently being restored by Clackmannanshire Heritage Trust. Phase 1, 2000, Simpson and Brown Architects, involved creating new roof structure, with temporary cladding, allowing structure to dry out (see p.4 and colour p.72). Excavations in 1984 and 1999 revealed cobbled surfaces, remains of an inner court, enclosing walls, elaborate drainage system, defensive ditch, turnpike stair and fragments of medieval glass, all being part of the substantial extension, about 80ft to west and north of the Tower, probably begun early 16th century. It is likely that the celebrated royal architect, William Schaw, who temporarily occupied his brother's house, would have extended these buildings in the 1580s–90s. Of the courtyard buildings, only the gallery wing to the west, dated 1631 on dormer windows, and misleadingly named **Old Sauchie House**, survived long enough to be photographed (colour p.72). The main house may yet be uncovered by excavation.

Sauchie was granted to Henri de Annand, kinsman to King Robert Bruce, in 1321, passing into the Schaw family a century later. The Schaws of Sauchie were among the most influential families of medieval Scotland. Sir James Schaw, Governor of Stirling Castle, refused James III access to his son and thus played a major role in the conspiracy that led to the king's murder at Sauchieburn in 1488. George Schaw, Abbot of Paisley, was Lord High Treasurer of Scotland in 1495 and the Schaws continued as Governors of Stirling Castle to James IV. The Schaw crest of three covered golden cups commemorates the hereditary post of Master of the Royal Wine Cellar granted to Alexander Schaw in 1529 and reconfirmed on his grandson by James VI. Alexander Schaw acquired the Greenock home of James Hamilton of Finnart (later called the Mansion House, see *South Clyde Estuary* in this series) upon the latter's forfeiture in 1540 and, paradoxically, it was another grandson, William Schaw, 1550–1602, who was later to inherit Finnart's own position at court of Master of Works.

William Schaw was for a while the inheritor of Sauchie during his brother's dispossession. He was the king's *Master of Works* responsible for work at Stirling Castle, Linlithgow, Holyrood and Dunfermline Abbey and probably Crichton and Castle Campbell, and was also responsible for developing Freemasonry in Scotland. In 1589–90 he was touring with James VI in Denmark. The Sauchie lands fell to a kinsman after George Schaw died without heir about 1690 and then passed, by his daughter's marriage in 1752, to the Cathcart family. William Schaw Cathcart, the 1st Earl, 1755–1843, was the most distinguished of a remarkable family of statesmen. As Russian Ambassador, his services were *of the greatest importance in the overthrow of Napoleon*. He retired to Britain but sold Schawpark to his sister's family, the Earls of Mansfield, in 1826. The house, offices and grounds still conveyed *the idea of decayed grandeur* in the mid-19th century but the house was unroofed in 1925 and finally demolished in 1961.

Old Sauchie House c.1880.

Top *Schawpark, 1910.* Above *The Cathcart family, Schawpark, by David Allan 1784; commemorating the first cricket match held in Scotland.* Right *Schawpark, Robert Adam's 1775 drawing of his proposed north front.*

In 1760, Bishop Pococke visited Schawpark: *The approach to it is round three sides of the plantations, and by a Village partly new built. Half a mile further stands the house of a very singular form …* He then describes its bow windows, battlements, cornice, pediments, balcony and square towers.

Auchinbaird Windmill.

In addition to manufacturing osnaburg (coarse linen originally from Germany) at Sauchie, Lord Cathcart encouraged the weaving of camblets (woollen garments). In 1775, he inherited **Schawpark**, planned to have the house remodelled by Robert Adam, but died before full plans could be implemented; what was achieved, with its odd gothic pavilions and windows, to a most unusual plan, demolished 1961 (colour p.73). Forestry Commission plantations on the estate and the golf course hide surviving evidence of an extensive designed landscape.

61 **Auchinbaird Windmill**, early 18th century
Originally built to harness wind power to drain a coal pit, converted to doocot at the pit's closure: rubble-built, circular tower with domed roof and castellated parapet, much the worse of time.

Devon Village, mid-19th century
Simple row of little-altered charming cottages.

62 **Devon Colliery Beam Engine House**, 1865
Tall, rectangular arched building of high-quality

workmanship, with arched openings and hipped slate roof. The engine, a Cornish pumping engine to drain the mineshaft, built by Neilson & Co. Cast-iron beam and pump have survived, but remainder removed for scrap metal. Beam Engine House sensitively restored, 1993, by Bob Heath Architect for the then district council, adding two mezzanine levels to provide offices for the council's ranger service above a meeting room, retaining the visual effect of a single-space interior, allowing for future removal of inserted work without damage. Excellent custom-built joinery (colour p.73).

Above and left *Devon Colliery Beam Engine House; top mezzanine.*

Dr John Roebuck, working with a Mr Eddison of Bo'ness, established the Devon Iron Works on Lord Cathcart's Schawpark estate, three miles north of Alloa, to exploit the rich seams of coal and ironstone. Two 40ft-high furnaces were built into a cliff above the Devon, just to the east of Sauchie Tower. The quarry face also supported the casting house and furnace air pump engine-house. Iron ore was imported and manufactured goods exported through Alloa. By 1842, ironstone was being obtained locally, while limestone was brought from South Queensferry. After a third furnace was built, the works produced about 6,000 tons of pig-iron per annum for the foundry which turned them into cast-iron goods for sale. The works closed in 1856.

FISHCROSS
Originally an 18th-century miners' row where Sheardale Ridge road crossed that between Alloa and Tillicoultry, part of which still remains along north side of Pitfairn Road. Gothic **Primary School** and **Schoolhouse**, 1887, Adam Frame. **Miners' Welfare Institute**, 1930, William Kerr, very similar to Sauchie Public Hall but smaller scale with Kerr's hallmarks of large bay windows and steep overhanging pitched roofs; needs careful restoration to reveal its potential.

Miners' Welfare Institute, Fishcross.

Gartmorn Dam, 1713 onwards
Oldest, and for many years largest, man-made reservoir in Scotland, built by the Earl of Mar to provide water power via a lade, to drain his coal mines at Holton (colour p.73).

63   Former **pump house** reverted to storage when Clackmannan District Council Architects designed a new visitor centre for the rangers at the entrance to dam.

Gartmorn provided the water that eventually gave Alloa the power for its industrialisation. A four-mile lade was constructed to bring water westwards to flood the marshy hollow of Gartmorn from the River Black Devon at Forestmill. The earthen dam has been rebuilt, and, until recent times, the 162-acre reservoir has provided Alloa, local breweries and distilleries with fresh water. The Gartmorn Country Park was recognised as a local nature reserve in 1980, for the 215-acre estate is an important nesting and wintering site for many species of wild fowl.

Pump house, Gartmorn Dam.

A **former resident** of Holton Square described her single end (one-room house) to Ian Adamson: *The room was very small and had a stone floor. Behind the door was a large shelf arrangement and taking up most of one wall was a range which in these days served as a cooker, clothes dryer for wet working clothes and room heater. Two double beds occupied most of the floor area, one was for the six children and the other was for the parents. There was little room for much else in the way of furniture than a wardrobe or dresser and of course a po' under the bed as there was no toilet or even running water in the house.*

Right Main Street, Sauchie c.1900. *Top* Sauchie Drill Hall. *Above* Sauchie Parish Church and Greycraigs House.

NEW SAUCHIE

Difficult to pinpoint a centre for this community as it bestrides the route from Alloa northwards. **Main Street**, having accordingly suffered usual road widening, may have lost whatever sense of containment it once had. **Sauchie Drill Hall**, built in 1819 as the Holton School, now housing (1992) and provides Sauchie with prominent landmark with its square castellated tower.

Burnbrae

Original miners' row lies on the east as Main Street turns uphill. **Keilarsbrae House**, *c*.1830, another good classical villa: well-cut stonework, doorway aggrandised by Doric pilasters and fine wrought-iron staircase inside. **Craigbank**, 1950s, W H Henry, County Architect, excellent scheme of terraces and low flats in brick with fashionable horizontal windows, portholes and door details. Gothic **Sauchie Parish Church**, 1841–2, David Rhind, designed to exploit commanding site with tall square tower at east end and parapeted pinnacled roof. Excellent internal woodwork. Adjacent 1872 **manse**. **Greycraigs House**, mid-19th century, similar to Keilarsbrae, though some 20 years younger.

Beechwood Nursing Home, 1999, Oliver and Robb Re-using the local name, this big nursing home is a long, friendly building set back from the main road. Two-storey bay windows and projecting pavilion provide rhythm to the frontage, with more detail in the textured blockwork and

Beechwood Nursing Home.

interest in the masonry claddings and strong blue-painted window frames. Site opposite for second nursing home by same architects.

66 **Sauchie Public Hall**, Fairfield Road, 1911; extended 1925, William Kerr
Jewel-like, red and white, Arts & Crafts hall, distinguished by its colour, overhanging steep-pitched roof, large multi-pane bay windows, leaded lights, recessed archway and buttresses – one of Kerr's best buildings.

Former Sauchie School, Mar Place, 1887, Adam Frame
Uneventful gothic, on site of Equity Court House (or *Ha'house*), established 1765 as a Baillie Court by the Erskines to settle disputes of the Holton mineworkers.

67 **United Free Church**, Church Grove, 1932, John Bruce
Simple harled brick church with reconstituted stone dressings, signalled by imposing square clocktower.

Top Sauchie Public Hall. Above United Free Church.

Left and below Sauchie Hospital.

Sauchie Hospital (Forth Valley Primary Care NHS Trust), Parkhead Road, 1893–5, John Melvin
Built as Combination Fever Hospital, it has pleasant entrance lodge and two-storey administration block which later absorbed the service accommodation behind. On either side, *entirely isolated ... for doubtful cases*, are two long single-storey male and female ward blocks *placed so that the wards will have as much of the sun as possible*. They still have good views over Sauchie. Detailing is *cottagey*: crested ridges, bay windows, wide-eaved dormers, margin-paned windows and timber-columned entrance porches to ward blocks (intended to double as verandas for convalescent patients). At the opening of the new observation block in 1937, the board chairman commented: *while we were one of the first infectious diseases hospitals in Scotland, we were about the last to substitute a motor for a horse ambulance.*

Auld Kirk.

Stewart Fowler

To the north of Tullibody Auld Kirk lie the remains of a stone coffin known as The Maiden Stone. Around 1450 the priest of Tullibody is said to have deceived Martha Wishart, the Maid of Myretoun, as to his intentions. On her deathbed, she instructed that her body was to be placed in a raised coffin by the church door, to shame the irreverent priest. The priest must have suffered, for he had the church door changed from the north to the south side.

Tullibody has its place in the history of the Reformation. Thomas Cocklaw, the last priest of the Catholic persuasion, adopted the principles of the reformers. On finding marriage warranted by the Scriptures, he took himself a wife, but the clergy retaliated by putting the attendants at his wedding to death. Cocklaw escaped with the Canon of Cambuskenneth to sanctuary in England; we are not told of the fate of his new wife.

TULLIBODY

Strategically positioned where the River Devon curves to meet the Forth at Cambus, Tullibody was the site of Kenneth mac Alpin's camp preceding his battle with the Picts near Cambuskenneth, 834 AD, which led to the uniting of the Kingdoms of the Scots and the Picts. After winning, Kenneth returned to Tullibody and erected a stone pillar as a memorial. In 1643, on the eve of his march to the battle of Kilsyth, the Marquis of Montrose quartered his men in Tullibody Woods, and while he dined with the Earl of Mar, his men *barbarously plundered* Alloa.

Circa 1800, the original clachan nestling around the Auld Kirk was removed, and the Abercromby laird laid out a new settlement on village riggs to the south. These new houses were round Main Street, most now demolished. In the late 19th century, the village expanded with the arrival of the tannery, and again in 1950s when Scottish Special Housing Association and the county council provided houses for the new miners.

68 **Auld Kirk**, Menstrie Road, 16th century
Little visible in the roofless remains can be traced to 1149 when David I granted the Lands and Inches of Tullibody to Cambuskenneth Abbey. Remains are those of rectangular 16th-century building which, after destruction by French army of Mary of Guise in 1559, fell into disrepair.

Restored and reroofed, 1760, George Abercromby, and presented with bellcote and old man-of-war ship's bell, and again restored in 1833, it was abandoned in 1904 as unsafe. Fine memorials include Corinthian-pilastered **frame** which once contained a tribute to the first laird, George Abercromby (1605–99), from Alexander Abercromby whom he adopted as his heir. Kirkyard includes interesting 18th-century monuments and unusual 1830 cast-iron memorial to James Donaldson of Devon Ironworks.

St Serf's Parish Church, 1904, Peter MacGregor Chalmers
Charmingly simple Romanesque with circular piers in north aisle, set back on grassy knoll overlooking the Devon Valley. Rubble stonework throughout and windows by Stephen Adams and Norman McDougall. The 1837 bell came from the Auld Kirk. **Church hall**, 1844, John Burnet, built as Tullibody's Free Church to *a superior design to many buildings for a similar object in this quarter* in pointed gothic. One of the earliest surviving buildings of John Burnet Sr, converted to church hall, 1951. The 1847 **manse** adjacent sternly classical.

Top *Abercromby Memorial, Auld Kirk.*
Above *St Serf's Parish Church.*

Left and below *The Tannery and Delph Pond, and the tannery workings, c.1910.*

69 **The Tannery**, Alloa Road, 1880 (colour p.73)
Large two-storey red brick block, with windows picked out in white brick, capped by further two storeys of windows and louvred timber ventilators, for through draughts and dissipation of stench. Founded c.1806 by Alexander Paterson, a shoemaker desiring to tan his own leather, it became the largest tannery in Scotland, dominated by top-heavy brick water tower. Bought by John Tullis in 1889, tanning continued until 1962, when it became a plastics factory. It took water from the Delph Pond, historically the common property of the village. Tanning pits infilled and currently being demolished in its entirety.

Top Main Street. *Above* The Nursery.

Tullibody School was famed for the high quality of its teachers, encouraged by the lairds. In 1794, Sir Ralph Abercomby wrote from Antwerp that a new school and schoolhouse be built. The schoolmaster of the time, Alexander Seggie, was so renowned a classical scholar that more young men from this school went to colleges than from the rest of the schools in Clackmannanshire put together.

Below Lych Gate. *Bottom* St Bernadette's RC Church.

Main Street

The heart of planned Tullibody lay south of Alloa Road, represented by Main Street straddling the route to Cambus. Not much of historic interest remains, the present centre being Tron Court, shopping precinct, 1967, W H Henry, County Architect, replacing decaying cottages. The **Tron Tree**, a lime planted by the well to mark the location of the public weighing machine, has gone, but at corner of **Delph Road** tree planted, 1902, by Mrs Robert Knox of Cambus, commemorates Edward VII's coronation. Attractive 19th-century houses and cottages in **Delph Road** are sole survivors of the 19th-century village: **No 11**, picturesque harled and pantiled cottage with stable (now garage) and **No 4**, simple classical house coated in dry-dash render.

School Road

Abercromby School, 1951, W H Henry
First post-war community school in the county, more like a village college: it originally contained maternity and child-welfare clinic and adult education provision as well as the primary school. Assembly hall block an exercise in bare geometrics. **The Nursery**, 1984, Central Regional Council Architects, takes the form of a glass-clad steel pyramid. **Old School Court**, 1995, Bracewell Stirling Architects, articulated continuous terrace of flats and disabled housing fronting School Road, provided by Ochil View Housing Association.

Lych Gate and War Memorial, 1921

At entrance to Tullibody Park, now lacking its inscribed panels. Large boulder known as *Samson's Button* or the *Haer Stane*, utilised as its base, into which was plugged a replica of the *Standin' Stane of Kenneth mac Alpin*, original destroyed, 1806.

St Bernadette's RC Church, Stirling Road, 1963, Peter Whiston
Modest rendered church for Tullibody expansion at corner of Baingle Brae uses double monopitches for hall and church, incorporating east-facing clerestory windows and flat-roofed columned porch to adjacent priest's house. Crucifixion mural by Donald Moodie.

70 **Baingle Brae**, 1834, Alexander Taylor (demolished *c*.1965)
Very fine towered villa built by Alexander Paterson of the Tannery following a trip to Italy, with similarities to The Vine (see *Dundee* in this series). Perhaps some Palladian country villa

Top *Floodlighting, Clackmannan Parish Church.* Above *Clackmannan.* Left *Clackmannan Colliery, c.1800, showing the water wheel, wagon road and coal workings, drawn by John Clerk of Eldin for Sir George Clerk of Penicuik.* Below left *Clackmannan Market Place.* Below *Kennetpans.*

Top *Clackmannan Tolbooth.* Top right
Brucefield House. Above *Alloa and The
Ochils from Clackmannan Hill.* Right
Postcard view of Alloa c.1940s. Below
Alloa in the 18th century by David Allan.

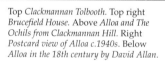

Andrew Millar

Bill Robertson

Bill Robertson

Top *Coalgate, Alloa*. Above *Tower Square from the east, with new entrance gatepier*. Left *Great Hall, Alloa Tower*. Below *Alloa Tower from south*.

Bill Robertson

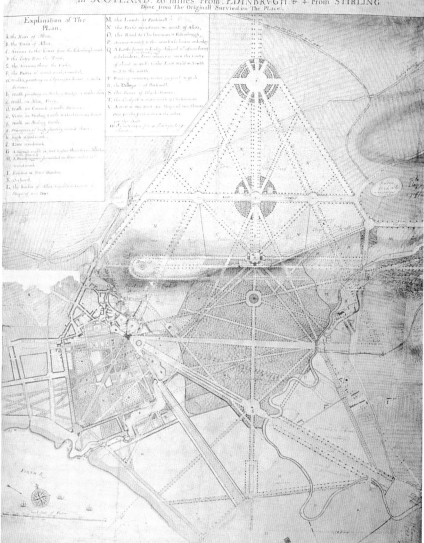

Plan of ALLOA: The Seat of The Lord MAR &c. In The Shire of CLACKMANAN In SCOTLAND. 26 milles From EDINBRVGH & 4 From STIRLING
Done from The Originall Survied on The Place.

Explanation of The Plan.

National Archives of Scotland (RHP 13258/1)

National Archives of Scotland (RHP 13258/11)

Above *Mar's Alloa estate plan of 1710–15, engraved by Bernard Lens. Each vista or walk centred on a distant landmark. The town and house are on the left; the parks, meadows and woods stretch towards Sauchie and Clackmannan. Present thinking is that it was almost entirely executed.*

Left *Front of Alloa Tower showing the two-bay addition and doubling of the entrance door (unexecuted). The Latin inscription means* Thus did the Lord Our God encourage our forefathers to bring forth the fruitfulness of this place. *This is an important clue to Mar's vision of Alloa as an ancient place renewed and prospering by the innovations of each generation.*

68

Top *Old Kirk and Mar and Kellie Mausoleum, Alloa.* Above left and middle *Broad Street Housing, Alloa; date plaque.* Left *Altar and stained glass, St John's Episcopal Church, Alloa.* Above *Bauchop's House, Alloa.*

Lys Hansen

RCAHMS
Bill Robertson

Law & Dunbar-Nasmith Architects

Top *For the people of Alloa: Writer, Artist, Music Maker/Join Hands with Brother Baker/Tis We Who Move the Earth* by Lys Hansen. Above *Thistle Brewery*. Middle *Kilncraigs Mill redevelopment*. Right *Staircase, Kilncraigs Mill office block*. Below *Mill Girls, Candleriggs, Alloa* by Lys Hansen.

Lys Hansen

George Sutherland

RCAHMS

Bill Robertson

Clackmannanshire Enterprise

Top left *Interior, former Alloa Public Baths (Speirs Centre).* Top *Front door, Fusco's, 69 Mill Street, Alloa.* Above *Hall, The Gean, Alloa.* Left *Orchard Lodge, The Gean.*

Top *Norwood and Cowdenpark, 1882 by W Adamson.* Middle *Old Sauchie House late 19th century.* Above *Stained glass, 15 Mar Street, Alloa.* Right *Caphouse, Sauchie Tower, during Phase 1 of restoration.* Below *Dunmar House Hotel, Alloa.*

Top and left *Devon Beam Engine House: mezzanines; section.* Top right *Gartmorn Dam.* Middle *Tullibody Tannery.* Above *Menstrie and the Ochils from Tullibody Tannery.* Below *Schawpark, Sauchie, late 19th century.*

Swan

Swan

Above *The Croft, mid-18th-century cottage on back road west of The Square, Blairlogie.* Right *Blairlogie Cottage.* Below *Cambus Iron Bridge.* Middle *Johnstone crest, Johnstone Mausoleum.* Bottom *Johnstone Mausoleum, Alva.*

Bill Robertson

Swan

Bill Robertson

Top *Surviving 1637 stone of St Serf's Church, Alva.* **Middle** *Cochrane Hall, Alva.* **Above** *Strude Mill, Alva.* **Left** *Scotland's Mill Trail Visitor Centre, Alva.* **Below** *Island Cottages, Alva.* **Bottom** *Co-op jubilee clock, Stirling Street, Alva.*

Top *Interior, Devonvale Hall, Tillicoultry.*
Above *Sterling Mills Designer Retail
Village.* Right *Former J & D Paton's Mill,
Tillicoultry.* Below *Jamieson Gardens,
Tillicoultry.* Below right *Ceiling detail,
Beechwood, Tillicoultry.*

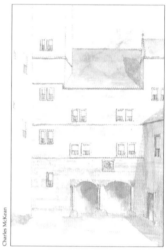

Top *Harviestoun Home Farm.* Left *Castle Campbell by R W Billings.* Above *Reconstruction drawing of Castle Campbell.* Below left *On the Burnside, Dollar c.1900.* Below right *Hillfoot House, Dollar.*

Top *Dollar Academy and Dollar from the golf course by Adam Robson.* Above *Mylne Bridge, Dollar, by Jennifer Campbell.* Right *Kellyside, Dollar.*

Below and right *Dollar Academy Gibson Music Building.* Bottom *Dollar Academy Gibson Music Building and Playfair Building.*

Top and left: *Ostlers, Kellybridge; interior courtyard.* Above *Mitchell Court, Dollar.* Below left *Ballroom fireplace, Solsgirth House, by Dollar.* Below *Dollarbeg, Dollar.*

79

Top left and right *Japanese Garden, Cowden, 1950s.*
Middle *Devonhall, Yetts o' Muckhart.* Left *Tollhouse,*
Dunning junction. Above *Middlehall, by Muckhart.*
Below *The Ochils by Oscar Goodall.*

Baingle Brae.

inspired the tall lantern tower and formal gardens. Seven acres of gardens, renowned for their beauty, lost with the house to the excited housing programme of the 1960s.

Tullibody House, *c.*1700, possibly by 6th Earl of Mar (demolished)
Tullibody House, on magnificent site by the shore, was the paternal seat of the Abercromby family, who later moved to Airthrey. Tall, old Scots house, plain and well ordered under steep, hipped roof, its grounds constantly improved according to the fashion of the time. The second George Abercromby was a leader in agricultural improvement and a founder of the Highland Society in 1784. Repaired, 1803, William Stirling. In the 19th century, vicinity became increasingly industrialised (something the Abercrombys might have seen as progress) and house demolished, early 1960s, as a result of railway works and vandalism.

The old house of Tullibody was built a few years before the Restoration by Mr Robert Meldrum … In point of shape it resembled the old house of Newton, being only larger. Mr Abercromby remembers it before his father demolished it to build the present house, which he set down in a corn ridge … His fir woods, taken off the moor, were enclosed and planted between 1725 and 1773 … In 1750 Tullibody was one of the neatest and best places in the country. It was, no doubt, in the very reverse of the present airy style. If, however, avenues and clipped hedges conveyed an idea of formality and constraint, they afforded shade and shelter both in heat and cold. And they were commonly disposed either to set capital objects in a striking point of view or to hide deformities … Perhaps I am partial to the place where I spent many of the happiest days of my youth – where I learned what no books can teach and where I formed my earliest friendships and views of life.
John Ramsay of Ochtertyre, MSS

John Abercromby, 1841–1924, 5th Lord Abercromby of Aboukir and Tullibody, retired from the army as lieutenant in 1870, and became a keen archaeologist and linguist. He was vice-president of the Folklore Society, president of the Society of Antiquaries of Scotland and an honorary member of the Finno-Ougrian Society, Helsinki, and of the Finnish Archaeological Society. He bequeathed an extensive library of volumes to Edinburgh University Library, along with notebooks, photographs and drawings.

Tullibody House.

Above and right *Tullibody House: wrought-iron balustrade; south porch.*

Robert Dick, 1811–66, was a native of Tullibody, his father an exciseman at Cambus and later Dall's Distillery, Glenochil. All his adult life he worked in poverty as a baker in Thurso, to support his studies into the natural sciences of the Caithness District. Hugh Miller, who received many geological and botanic specimens from Dick, wrote that *he has robbed himself to do me service.*

The lands of orchard of Tullibody are mentioned in a charter of 1521, but the old house was not long built in 1655 when Robert Meldrum sold it to George Abercromby, 1625–99, who came from Skein in Aberdeenshire. Alexander, 1675–1754, the second laird, was from Birkenbog, Banffshire, and was only a near relative who had lived with George since childhood. *A warm supporter of the Hanoverian Succession, he was a rigid Presbyterian*, and it was he who rebuilt the house and laid out the grounds, acquiring Menstrie Castle in 1719. His son, George, 1705–1800, second of Tullibody, one-time Professor of Law at Edinburgh University, was the laird who brought fame to the estate. A noted improver, he lived to the age of 95: to see his first son knighted, Sir Ralph Abercromby, 1734–1801, later hero of the battle of Aboukir Bay in which he was killed; his second son knighted, Sir Robert Abercromby, Governor of Bombay; and his third son, Alexander, as Lord Abercromby, a Law Lord in the Court of Session. In his later years George retired to Brucefield, leaving Tullibody to Sir Ralph, who had been living at the family's third seat, Menstrie.

Tullibody Old Bridge, (*below*) Bridgend, Stirling Road, *c*.1535 and 1697
Unusually long, 442ft, and varying in width from 20ft to 11½ft, the bridge has two principal arches over the river and three flood arches to the west (the Devon is prone to flooding at this point). At the main crossing point, this bridge had its eastern arch broken down by Kirkcaldy of Grange, 1559. One of several bridges erected in the neighbourhood of Stirling by Robert Spittal, philanthropist and Royal tailor (see *Stirling and The Trossachs* in this series). Now in urgent need of restoration, with potential new use as part of the National Cycle Route.

71 Doocot, New Mills Crossing, 17th century
In a field near the bridge, lean-to doocot in sad
state of repair, with crumbling crowstepped walls
containing a fair number of nesting boxes.

CAMBUS

Cambus (a creek or haven) is situated at the
confluence of the River Devon with the Forth.
A dam was built on the Devon to drive corn and
barley mills on each side of the river, and a pier
was built to allow flat-bottomed boats to deliver
and receive the grain and flour. For years there
was a flourishing salmon industry, which
declined owing to pollution of the two rivers.
Beer had been brewed at Cambus for centuries
before Robert Knox established his brewery in
1786, but Cambus is probably more noted for its
distillery and bonding sheds, founded, 1806, by
John Moubray. The 19th-century distillery was
burnt down in 1914 and totally rebuilt, 1937–8.
Only part of the **still-house tower** remained to
give the present building some connection with
the past. Complex still used for blending and
storage, but no longer distils. Fine example of

Tullibody was seen by contemporaries
as a centre of enlightenment and
intelligence in an Arcadian setting.
Witness the memory of John Ramsay of
Ochertyre who referred to it as the *loved
haunt of my youth*. He visited it again, as
an old man in 1803: *I was glad to see the
house so much improved, yet so much like
what it was in the cheerful morn of my
youth*. In 1809, he recorded after another
visit: *Our entertainment was good but not
overloaded or overdressed, and I have
seldom seen a second course more honoured
in the eating. Even I ate some fritters not to
be particular ... the conversation was very
good ... the house is a good one and much
improved and without doors ... everything
is gay and well disposed. Plenty of gravel
walks and good roads ...*

Glenochil, Cambus and Carsebridge
distilleries were three of the six lowland
grain distilleries which amalgamated in
1877 to form Distillers Company Limited.

New Mills Doocot.

In 1814, twenty *ca'ing* whales swam
aground at Cambus and were killed.
James Hogg immortalised (and
exaggerated) the tragedy thus:
  *Ane hundred and threttye bordlyie whailis
    Want snorying up the tydde.
  And wyde on Allowais fertylle holmis
    They gallopit ashore and died.*

Left *Cambus*. Below and bottom
Cambus Distillery.

In 1697, John, 6th Earl of Mar, agreed with Mason Thomas Bauchop (father of famous Alloa Master Mason Tobias, who witnessed the document) that *the said Thomas shall construct and build a new arch at the east end of the bridge of Tullibody, finish the gate, and mend the pear of the mid pillars thereof, and to bat it with iron, mend the calsie of the whole bridge and to put on a tirlace gate, with lock and key thereto ...* It is uncertain how much of the present structure is Spittal's bridge and how much Bauchop's.

After Kirkcaldy of Grange had broken down the bridge to hinder the Queen Regent's French Army, the latter improvised with the now Protestant kirk roof instead. According to John Knox: *The French, expert anouch sicne factis tuik don the roofe of a parish church and maid a brig over the watter called Dovane and so they aschapit and came to Striveling and syne to Leith.*

early 19th-century **cast-iron bridge** leads from the distillery to the east bank of the Devon, appropriately rescued and restored, 1995, Clackmannan District Council, repaired by Ted Ruddock. Repainted using authentic paints and colours but prone to harmless discolouration caused by whisky fungus (colour p.74).

The village, on the banks of the Devon, is a surprisingly hidden cluster of cottages, most from 19th century – with pantile roofs, skews and random rubble walls – or from W H Henry's 1950s' reconstruction programme. Easternmost house is grander, with 1743 marriage stone.

Lornshill Farmhouse, *c.*1770
Striking classical farmhouse on south side of Tullibody to Alloa road, plain beneath steep, hipped roof, save for bay windows and Venetian doorway (round headed flanked by narrow rectangular windows).

Top *Lornshill Farmhouse*. Right *King o' Muirs Farmhouse*. Above *Middleton Kerse*.

King o' Muirs is associated with James V who, in one of his wanderings incognito as the Gudeman of Ballengeich, was offered hospitality by one Donaldson, then tenant. Ballengeich suggested that Donaldson might visit him at Stirling Castle, where he discovered his guest to have been the king. The king presented him with the title *King of the Muirs*. The last Donaldson of King o' Muirs moved to Alloa, where it is said King Street was named after him.

King o' Muirs Farmhouse, near Glenochil, late 18th century
Plain two-storey harled farmhouse with hipped slate roof and bowed centre window. At **Glenochil**, detention centre built, 1966, on site of failed 1952 Glenochil Mine; became Young Offenders' Institution, 1976. Its sheeting roofs and monopitch forms of nearby housing look more impressive from a distance.

Middleton Kerse, between Glenochil and Menstrie, early 19th century
Large classical mansion with belvedere, by James Meiklejohn, an Alloa brewer. Bought by McNabs of Glenochil Distillery, 1871, it had a walled garden, unusually with undersoil heating. Demolished 1965.

THE HILLFOOTS

Sheltered in the lee of the Ochil Hills lie the
Hillfoots villages of Blairlogie, Menstrie, Alva,
Tillicoultry and Dollar. Each village grew around
a fast-flowing burn, necessary for water and
power for the meal mills and later woollen mills.
The villages of Alva and Tillicoultry developed as
small industrial textile towns. Each village usually
enjoyed the patronage of a laird on whose ground
it was built and who resided nearby. The old 1669
Statute Labour Act road from Stirling to Kinross
passed through each village some way up the
slope, and sections of it are still in use. In each
village, the oldest cottages can be found at this
level, some way uphill of the 1806 turnpike road.

BLAIRLOGIE

Just west of the Clackmannanshire boundary, this
tiny village is the first of the Hillfoots settlements,
sheltering beneath Dumyat where the Ochils are
at their most precipitous (see *Stirling and The
Trossachs* in this series).

72 **Blairlogie Castle**, 1546, Alexander Spittal
Small tower house with 1582 east wing. Original
tower has unusual stairturret corbelled out at
south-east corner, main roof and crowstepped
gable continuing over and around. Initials A S
and E H on dormer windows those of Alexander
Spittal and his wife Elizabeth Hay, in whose
family it remained until 1767. Legend accords it a
secret chamber.

Since early last century each Hillfoots
burgh has been ascribed a distinguished
name: Alva – *The Model Burgh* after its
model lodging house; Tillicoultry – *The
Fountain Burgh* after its numerous
fountains, and also *The Floral Burgh* in
tribute to its displays of roses that lined
the main streets; and Dollar – *The Classic
Burgh* after its academy.

Below and bottom *Blairlogie Castle.*

Right *Hillside and Crowsteps*. Below *Montana Cottage*. Middle *Village hall*. Bottom *Sundial, Crowsteps*.

Blairlogie has had a reading room since the 18th century, though perhaps not always in the same building. The reading room now forms the nucleus of the village hall, being originally one of the single-storey cottages, gifted to the village at the beginning of the 20th century by the Hares of Blairlogie House. In 1947 the reading room committee bought the adjacent two-storey cottage (Crowsteps) and extended the reading room into it.

The village, *c.*1750–1900, forms a picturesque group of cottages in the lee of the castle, and promoted itself as a health resort. Villagers maintained a herd of about 50 goats, whose milk was tuberculosis free and ideal for consumptives, and rented out accommodation to visitors; the brisk mountain air was considered a bonus. The old High Road from Stirling to Kinross debouches into Blairlogie at a picturesque square, closed at the top by **Montana Cottage**, dated 1765. Overhanging pantile roof, fine Italianate pilastered doorpiece and unusual oriel window represent an early 20th-century remodelling and extension. Date stone to one side of the window has the initials J A and I T: on the other side is a sundial. Garage on east side of the square used as goat-milking parlour in 18th and 19th centuries, the goats being kept on 'Goat's Green' immediately behind Montana Cottage.

On the old road to the east of the square are 18th-century cottages, revitalised, 1970s, Duncan Stirling: **Hillside**, 1976, formed from two previously derelict cottages; **village hall**, 1975, combination of three 18th-century cottages – **Crowsteps**, two-storey cottage with outside stair, slate roof, crowsteps and sundial set into the wall, and adjoining pair of low pantiled cottages – provides large space for village functions. Hall incorporates village's historic **reading room**.

West of the square, **Blairlogie Cottage**, (colour p.74) whitewashed, 18th century, with hipped slate roof and, adjoining, 1979 hexagonal **Watergate Cottage** by Duncan Stirling. The old **watergate** to the now overgrown well has been preserved as a feature.

Left *Blairlogie and Watergate Cottages, with watergate in foreground.* Above *Blairlogie United Free Church.*

Blairlogie United Free Church, 1846
Plain with three pairs of double gothic windows and bellcote adjoining grander 1865 **manse**.
Kirklea Cottage, 1758 datestone re-used, formed from row of thatched and pantiled tiny cottages.
Struan has a row of eccentric gothic windows painted on its elongated dormer window.
Puddleduck's Tearoom, former post office, harled with sandstone architraves. Panel, built into small south wing, bearing trade emblems of a carpenter, dated 1728, and initialled I T and H B, removed from a cottage demolished when nearby classical **Telford House** was built, *c*.1870. Carpenter was John Telford, whose family owned the surrounding land. A later member was William Telford, one of seven founding partners of Stirling's first private bank in 1777. **Fenham**, off main road, east of the village, 1986 adaptation of quaint old Boghead.

Powis House, 1746–7
Tall Scots mansion, with ashlar quoins and window dressings, and Adam-style interiors on the site of Powhouse, home of the Stirlings of Herbertshire. Stable block, with octagonal-roofed doocot, converted to housing by Duncan Stirling.

Blairlogie had the first congregation of the newly formed Presbytery of Relief in 1740. *Last Tuesday there was a numerous meeting of followers of the Seceding Presbytery upon the hill near Logie; but the people from the neighbourhood went up against them in battle array and, breaking their tents to pieces, dismissed them. They then repaired to Kippenross Muir near Dunblane where they erected a tent with plaids. Messrs Ebenezer and Ralph Erskine, Moncrieff and Nairn, with another gentleman were present.*
The Caledonian Mercury, 30 April 1740
On 16 June 1762, Messrs Gillespie, Boston and Colier met as a Presbytery at Blair-Logie. This was practically teaching the people of Scotland how they might secure their religious rights and privileges, for if the people of a small village of Blair-Logie could rear a church and voluntarily support religious ordinances among themselves, no oppressed parish need brook church and state enactment.
Gavin Struthers, from *The History of the Rise, Progress and Principles of the Relief Church*, 1848

The congregation built themselves a church in 1762, but this was destroyed by fire in 1845. The new church cost £630 and had 200 sittings. It became Blairlogie United Presbyterian Church in 1847 and then, three name changes later, Blairlogie United Free Church in 1954.

Left *Kirklea Cottage.* Below *Telford House.*

The Orchard comprised three 18th-century cottages to the west of Blairlogie Park. The last occupied cottage narrowly missed being flattened when an immense boulder came crashing down from a precipice above on Castle Law in August 1935. It was replaced by a timber bungalow in 1943, which unfortunately was hit by a second severe rockfall in 1948. All that remains is the huge boulder in what is now the picnic area.

Dumyat
I can scarcely conceive nobler prospects than there are from that mountain, wrote Lord Cockburn in 1838. *It is one of the many places which make us not at all afraid to boast of Scotland, even in comparison with Switzerland. Our solitude and elevation derived an additional charm from the distant view of the people sweltering below at the Stirling races.*

Robert Anderson, a native of Tullibody, ran away to sea, having *got a girl with child.* He made his fortune as a shipmaster, trading in Spain, where he was joined by his brother-in-law, Edward Mayne of Cambus. Mayne's nephew Edward inherited most of the wealth, and he used this to build Powis House.

Only an attractive row of miners' housing commemorates **Manor**, an ancient defensive post and landing on the Forth. *Manor, or Kingsnow House, has been a Roman station, some vestiges of the trenches being lately visible. It was part of the lordship of Stirling and feued by the Callenders about 1479.* Ralph Dundas, grandfather of John Ramsay of Ochertyre, who wrote the above, was the last to live at Manor, his successor abandoning the old house, or castle, in 1729 to build *a small snug house at Airthrey* in 1747. He soon sold it to the Haldanes, patrons of Robert Adam (see *Stirling and The Trossachs* in this series), from *the want of proper relish for a country life.* Ironically, Robert Haldane resold the estate about 1796 to Dundas' nephew, Sir Robert Abercromby, and Airthrey subsequently succeeded Tullibody as the Abercromby seat.

Menstrie from the slopes of Dumyat.

Blairlogie Park
Classical villa in dressed stone, service wing behind, set where the hillside is at its steepest.

73 **Blairlogie House** (*above*)
Rambling gothicised Victorian country house, previously hotel, developed out of 18th-century Montague Cottage. One-time owners Colonel Ian Hare and his wife Alice celebrated by monogrammed fireplace and the Colonel's ghost is said to *so enjoy* the house, it is reluctant to leave. Sheriff John Tait and Archibald Campbell Tait, Archbishop of Canterbury, (sons of Craufurd Tait of Harviestoun) also owned it, as a country cottage for visits home, leaving a burden on later owners to look after Tait's Tomb (see p.114).

74 **Redcar**, 1880
Built for Sheriff T B Johnstone, sits high above the road amid mature rhododendrons. Gothic, with half-hipped and pitched red-tile roofs, decorated ridge and paired windows. It cost about £2,000 to blast a platform for the house out of the hillside, but the unsurpassed view presumably made it worthwhile.

MENSTRIE

Small village with double origin: partly based on the castle and its estate on the rich Forth carseland and partly on woollen manufacture.

Menstrie Castle.

75 Menstrie Castle, late 16th century
Sturdy, picturesque, three-storey L-plan castellated house (never a castle). It is the rump of a full inner court, entered through a wide-arched pend, and what survives is probably not the principal house of the complex. After centuries of neglect and misuse as a tenement, saved from demolition by a campaign led by the actor Moultrie Kelsall; steep roof, crowstepped gables, dormer windows and pepperpot turrets all restored, 1961. It thus represents a large wealthy manor house, entirely indefensible, being surrounded by hills. Now domesticated by its claustral setting amidst W H Henry's pleasant 1957–60 square of housing, it would originally have formed an impressive sight amidst these Forth flatlands. Contains a commemoration room to the Baronets of Nova Scotia, administered by the National Trust for Scotland, in recognition of the castle as birthplace of Sir William Alexander, founder of Nova Scotia.

Main Street

Effectively splits Menstrie into old and new. To the south lie the principal housing estates: those of the 1950s and '60s to the west, those of the 1970s and '80s to the east. Latter associated with nearby **Glenochil Yeast Factory**, where UDV / Diageo is building its national archive centre. Splendid **Menstrie Primary School**, 1978, Central Regional Council Architects, a warren of little classrooms and workspaces leading off communal central areas. **Holly Tree Hotel** refaced, 1950s, in Thirties style – reconstituted stone with horizontal windows, the door

The Alexanders had been granted Menstrie *c*.1500. It was probably during the youth of William Alexander, the statesman born at Menstrie in 1567, that this great new house was built. In 1584 he was appointed travelling companion to the eight-year-old Earl of Argyll on the latter's travels on the Continent. He subsequently ingratiated himself with the young James VI by his poetry, on which he prided himself in endless philosophical strophes *in the manner of the Ancients*. He moved to England with the king in 1603, became tutor to Prince Henry and was knighted in 1609. In 1625 he became Lieutenant of Nova Scotia and the following year, principal Secretary for Scotland. He was reviled, suspected of debasing the Scots coinage and, despite his elevation to Viscount Stirling and the creation of a splendid new town house in Stirling itself (see *Stirling and The Trossachs* in this series), he died a bankrupt.

Moultrie R Kelsall, 1901–80, actor and producer, appeared in many 1950s' classic films, and also launched campaigns to save historic buildings including Provost Skene's House and Provost Ross's House, Aberdeen (see *Aberdeen* in this series), and Menstrie Castle. In 1961 he and architect Stuart Harris wrote *A Future for the Past*, an early conservation manual showing how abandoned buildings could be made into comfortable homes. His home, Kirklea Cottage, Blairlogie (see p.87), is the first case study.

Holly Tree Hotel.

*O' Alva woods are bonnie;
Tillicoultry hills are fair,
But when I think o' the bonnie braes
o' Menstrie
It makes my heart aye sair.*
Ancient rhyme

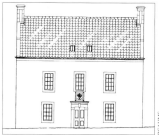

Top *Midtown*. Middle *Windsor Castle*. Above *Menstrie House*. Right *Elmbank Mill*.

James Holburne, a general in the Scots army against Cromwell, acquired Menstrie from Alexander's creditors in 1649, and his family, who sold the estate to the Abercrombys in 1719, is remembered by its coat-of-arms panel at Midtown – the site of Windsor Castle. The last member of the family, Miss Mary Anne Barbara Holburne (d.1882), of Bath, left part of her estate to endow Menstrie Parish Church, and with the remainder founded the Holburne of Menstrie Museum in Bath.

Menstry was feued from the Argyll family by the father of the first Earl of Stirling. This nobleman had an uncommon share of taste for his time. He made a terrace walk from Myreton to Playgreen, which commanded a delightful prospect of the Forth and the country around … In the Civil Wars the house with its battlements was burnt by the Covenanters. It was rebuilt by the Holburnes, one of whom, about 1700, planted an excellently assorted orchard.
John Ramsay of Ochtertyre, MSS

becoming part of the surround of the horizontal window above, while single-storey parapeted bay window curves round south-west corner. Remains of gable disguises the flat roof. **Cost Cutter** now occupies Co-operative Society Grocery, ornamented by exquisite two-face, triangular clock dated 1897, in celebration of Co-op's 50th jubilee. **Parish church** and **hall**, 1880, James Collie, narrow, long Victorian gothic rectangles, with steep-pitched roofs, decorated at ridge line, and low buttressed side walls.

Midtown, W H Henry
Group of cottage-inspired old people's housing overlooking the landscaped area around the burn, on site of **Windsor Castle**, likely dower house of Menstrie Castle. End house has coat-of-arms panel of the Holburne family, with the motto *Decus meum virtus,* inserted in gable end. Opposite, **Menstrie House**, 1982, Central Regional Council Architects, more old people's housing near the burn: large rendered wings with red-tile hipped roofs and sitting areas identified by red-stained corner conservatories, whose rugged views contrast with the neat landscaping.

76 **Elmbank Mill**, *c.*1865
Long, rectangular and rubble built, north façade reminiscent of small Georgian country house, once part of much larger complex founded by George Drummond as gas-powered woollen mill, 1864, the boom period of Menstrie's textile industry; rest demolished, early 1970s. Drummond was joined and then succeeded by James Johnstone (builder of Broomhall). Now business centre. To the east is **Brook Street**, series of single-, two- and three-storey housing blocks in red brick for Ochil View Housing Association, completed 2000, James F Stephen. Interest is in the details, dormers on cottage blocks and vertical bay windows on the high blocks.

Left Brook Street. *Above* United Presbyterian Mission Hall.

100-102 and 104-106 Main Street

Almost identical gothic cottages with porches, bay windows and canted dormer windows, with wrought-iron finials. **United Presbyterian Mission Hall**, 1891, Adam Frame, also gothic, but of pleasing proportions; porch has moulded arch and stone cross finial.

Ochil Road

Former main street retaining a few 18th- and 19th-century cottages continues into **New Row**. Rest rebuilt in W H Henry's pretty, sympathetic post-war style, which strove to find an acceptably modern Scottish idiom. **Auld Brig**, 1665, rubble-built, humpback, single arch with inscribed panel on the south. Stone walls of 1642 corn mill can yet be spotted, just above Auld Brig.

In 1800 John Ramsay re-visited Menstrie, where he had spent much time in the summer of 1752–3 *in my cheerful morn of youth when Mr Abercromby and his wife lived there in great credit and felicity.* He found *the staircase up to the drawing room ruinous and everything bore the marks of desolation … the rooms where hospitality and kindness once abode were waste or full of lumber.*

Left Burnside and Auld Brig c.1900. Below Broomhall.

77 **Broomhall**, 1874, John Forbes, succeeded by Francis Mackison
Splendid castle-like mansion, built for James Johnstone of Elmbank Mill, latterly used as Clifford Park boys' boarding school, burnt out in 1940. It long stood empty as a magnificent hillside ruin, but was redeveloped as a nursing home, 1988, by Bracewell Stirling Architects; now seeking new use (see p.4). Lodge, boundary walls and gatepiers survive, stables converted to house, 1977.

MENSTRIE

Menstrie played a small but significant role in establishing the textile industry in the Hillfoots. In 1800 the three Archibald brothers from Tullibody built their first woollen mill on the site between Menstrie Burn and Brook Street. One of them, John, had (with his sons) introduced the first local steam-powered machinery at Menstrie.

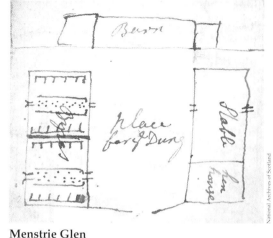

It was from the **Myretoun** in September 1804 (then tenanted by his sister Mrs Thomson) that the famous African explorer, **Mungo Park**, 1771–1806, set off on his second expedition to the African interior on which he died.

Menstrie Glen

Now mostly deserted to sheep and hillwalkers, the glens cutting through the southern escarpment of the Ochils are rich with archaeological remains. Menstrie Glen's few medieval sheep farms gave way to densely farmed and settled status by the mid-18th century with about 22 farms – boundaries, plantings, yards and building remains survive. The reversion to sheep farming and agricultural improvements, with significant enclosures and plantings, was instigated by James Wright, 1730–69, of Loss, who owned half the glen, became wealthy enough to purchase Argyll's Lodging, Stirling (see *Stirling and the Trossachs* guide) and left records of his improvements. The modern landscape of the glen is as much a product of human management as the carse below.

Loaningbank, on the back road to Alva, is a group of farm buildings; white-rendered cottage is West Loaningbank and to east are dilapidated rubble and pantile buildings characteristic of past prosperity. **Damsburn House**, nearby, very neat three-bay, two-storey refurbished rubble house with low west range and date stone *1785/1985*, takes its name from the burn, once dammed to turn a mill wheel. **The Myretoun**, behind, ancient fermtoun, said to date from 13th century. Present Victorianised house from 1761 was dower house for Alva estate until bought by the Porteous family of Meadow Mill, 1940. **Balquharn** still has farm buildings but predominantly vast white-rendered pavilion – a 1980s' ranch house for owner of local construction company.

ALVA

Centre of historic Alva, as with all Hillfoots communities, is uphill from the main road (Stirling Street) where the old road (Back Road, Beauclerc Street, Ochil Road) crosses the Alva Burn at the entrance to the Glen. Parish church was to the east on the edge of the community. Clustered round the burn – Green Square, Erskine Street, Beauclerc Street, the Island and Brook Street – one finds traces of old Alva, whose origins derive partly from the influence of the great lairds of Alva House, to the east, and partly to the mills, the finest of which, Strude Mill, stands silhouetted against the hills, dominating the entire town.

Opposite from top *Loss Farm by James Wright, 1750s; Cottages at Damsburn and probably Loaningbank, late 19th century, indicating there was a sizeable community east of Menstrie, along the old main road; The Myretoun c.1900; Part of extensive distillery warehousing at Glenochil, stretching east from The Yeast Factory (see p.89), mostly screened from the road, but when visible said to be the richest view in Scotland.*

Alva House (demolished)

A tower house, certainly extant in 1542, was incorporated into Sir Charles Erskine's new mansion of 1636, which in turn became the east wing of Alva House when the Johnstones added the huge south front and west wing *c.*1820. Miss Carrie Johnstone inherited the house and estate in 1890 and, although still fondly remembered for her kindness, she overspent so considerably that on her death in 1929, the sale of the estate and house contents did not pay her debts. The house could not be sold and eventually collapsed during the war

Top *Alva House and Sauchie Tower drawn by Anthony Stuart, 1790.* Above *Alva House.*

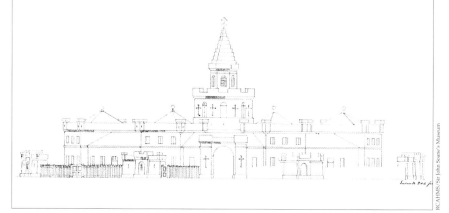

Swan

Swan

Top *Castellated stable block as proposed for Alva House by Robert and James Adam, 1789.* Middle *Farriers Hotel.* Above *Alva House Walled Garden.*

The first Erskine of Alva, Sir Charles, a younger son of the 2nd Earl of Mar, bought the estate in 1636 and became keeper of Cambuskenneth Abbey which had been granted to the 1st Earl at the Reformation (see *Stirling and The Trossachs* in this series). Erskine's son, also Sir Charles, became a Baronet of Nova Scotia in 1666 and had four remarkable sons. The eldest, Sir James, was killed at the Battle of Landen in 1693. **Sir John Erskine**, 1672–1739, a Jacobite, is remembered for his discovery of an *exceedingly rich* vein of silver in the hills above Alva, from which he had extracted the value of about £4,000 per week, from 1710, to which he owed his pardon for his part in the 1715 Jacobite uprising. *He was a man of more genius than conduct, of more wit than wisdom*, wrote John Ramsay of Ochtertyre, *but the heat and volatility of his fancy would not be regulated by prudential considerations.*

when used for military target practice. The family is still represented through other branches of the Johnstones.

House was situated in beautiful surroundings, high on wooded hillside, embracing extensive views. Pleasure grounds included long formal avenues, to east and west, fountains, terraces, flower gardens and rare trees. Plans were prepared by Robert and James Adam in 1789 to refront the house and build a castellated **stable block**, but the only built part of the project seems to have been the Johnstone Mausoleum.

79 **Farriers Hotel** and **Ochil Crafts**, 1805–9, probably by William Stirling
Formerly Alva House stables, symmetrical rectangular courtyard block with projecting towers to centre and wings of frontage. Ground floor provided stabling for 17 horses as well as two coach houses, harness rooms and later, garage accommodation. First-floor housing for coachman, butler, gamekeeper and grooms. Originally a doocot above arched central carriageway entrance. Now beautifully restored and converted, 1990, McEwan Builders, to hotel and restaurant, retaining original elevations.
Ochil Hills Woodland Park, formed from woodlands of Alva House estate, now provides waymarked forest walks and still has 18th-century **ice house**.

Alva House Walled Garden, 1999, Montgomery Forgan
The 19th-century kitchen garden now provides enclosure for large neo-Palladian contemporary villa in brown stone, contrasting with aged brick of garden walls. Huge pedimented slender-columned portico dominates but windows and odd extra bay to the east spoil its proportions. It controls the hillside, yet close up is hidden by steep incline and garden wall. It will be much enhanced when planting matures.

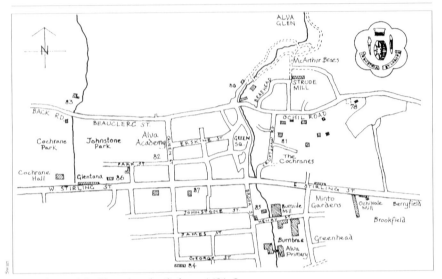

St Serf's Parish Church, rebuilt from 1631–2
Plain Georgian, with gothic ornamentation
representing an 1815 rebuilding probably by
William Stirling, which incorporated 1632
sanctuary. Victorian additions included twin low
square towers in re-entrant angles. In 1981,
congregation merged with Alva, and St Serf's,
badly affected by dry rot, was abandoned.
Damaged by fire, 1985, subsequently demolished
(colour p.75).

St Serf's Parish Church.

78 **Johnstone Mausoleum**, 1790, Robert and
James Adam
Small, square groin-vaulted building of two
storeys, memorials being on the upper. Entrance
arch framed by Doric columns supporting
triangular pediment; empty pedimented niches
in north and south walls. Johnstone crests on the
gates originally on gates to Alva House, removed
to Johnstone Park when house demolished, later
reset here (colour p.74).

Sir John Erskine's neighbour, probably
Abercromby of Tullibody, remarked of
his estate improvements: *Sir John, all this
is very fine and practicable, but it would
require a princely fortune*, to which the
reply: *George, when I first formed my
scheme of policy for this place, I was
drawing such sums out of the mine that I
could not help looking upon the Elector of
Hanover as a small man.* His ambitious
projects, which included a canal
between the Devon and his coal mines,
and extensive agricultural enclosures
and improvements, absorbed most of
his wealth. His son, Sir Henry, the 5th
Baronet, was a fashionable figure in
London political circles, said by Horace
Walpole to be *a military poet and a
creature of Lord Bute's.* The Alva
baronetcy ended with Sir John's
grandson, Sir James Erskine, who
succeeded his maternal uncle as 2nd
Earl of Rosslyn in 1805.

Johnstone Mausoleum.

Top *Island House*. Middle *The Island*. Above *Braehead*. Right *Strude Mill and Robertson Street*.

Of Sir John's brothers, **Robert Erskine**, 1677–1718, was physician to Peter the Great of Russia, and **Charles Erskine**, 1680–1763, Lord Tinwald, afterwards Lord Justice Clerk, bought the Alva Estate about 1749 from his nephew. Ramsay noted that he was *one of the most distinguished characters of those times*, but that *A fastidious critic might think there was sometimes too much art and finesse in his way of expressing himself.* Lord Tinwald's son James was also Lord Justice Clerk, taking the name Lord Barjarg, and later Lord Alva, the last Erskine of Alva.

The Boll, or Strude Mill bell is preserved at The Cochranes (see p.98), with a Lallans inscription (1963) by Alva poet James Nicol Jarvie:
For a hunner year an mair it was this bell
that waukened the Douce A'va folk
Airly Ilka Mornin, binna the Sabbath Til
Anither Darg and lowsd' Them Ilka nicht.
Aa that time the Bell hung heigh on the
Boll Mill Bot or it micht faa.
It wis brocht doon an stans here
Among folk that anes Kenn'd it weel:
Its auld tongue, Quate Noo is
Bot a Ghaist-soond i' mony an A'va Memory.

Alva Glen
Attractive nature walk of tree-lined paths carved out of steep rock faces and narrow bridges over steep gorges. At entrance to Alva Glen is the Eadie Memorial Fountain.

Island House, 16 Brook Street, mid-18th century Reputed to have been the first house in Alva taller than a single storey, and thereby christened *The Castle*. Two storeys of local whinstone, walls 2ft thick, the house sat guarding entrance to the glen and provided four very crowded dwellings of one or two rooms each. Absorbed by Cunningham's Longbank Printworks, 1930s, now Stephen Clark Fabrications. **The Island**, (colour p.75) is a row of harled and slated cottages by the Alva Burn; easternmost was the smithy of Robert Porteous, grandfather of the builder of Meadow Mill. **Braehead**, 1938, Burgh Architect, flat-roofed terraces of stepped two-storey houses, ascending hillside to the Strude Mill. Uniformity of colour now partly spoilt by personalisation of owner occupiers. Excellent re-use of historic street lamp standards with less interesting contemporary lanterns.

Strude (or Boll) Mill, *c.*1820 (colour p.75)
The glory of Alva. Beyond places like New Lanark, Scottish mills rarely rose to the classical dignity of this six-storey, 25-window long mill, in squared rubble with dressed stone. Its commanding presence is emphasised by the central four bays being capped by a pediment and bellcote. It was only part of a larger group of mill buildings owned by William Archibald & Son until 1976. At each window was a handloom but the tradition that there were 365 windows, one for each day of the year, is over optimistic. Converted to flats, 1987.

Robertson Street is a row of 1870s' weavers' cottages, running north to Strude Mill. Cottages along **Ochil Road** are 19th-century remnants of Alva's first ribbon development. Houses along south side are mill owners' 19th-century mansions with large gardens and outbuildings. **Manse**, 1950s, on old site (original, 1810–12, William Stirling); **Glenside** and **Balnagowan**, late Victorian gothic mansions. **Craigknowe**, 1939–40, one of William Kerr's last commissions, white-harled brick cottage with little dormers in rambling slate roof, bay window to sitting room, quite isolated within steep terraced garden overlooking Devon Valley, at end of long tree-lined drive squeezed from a neighbouring garden. Gothic **Ochilbank**, 1820, built for the Johnstone family as a home for a younger son (James Raymond Johnstone having 16 children), extended *c.*1860. **Kenmuir**, 1813, and **Bernard Cottage**, two-storey, white-harled Georgian.

Top *Craigknowe*. Above *Ochilbank*.

Edgehill.

Croftshaw Road

Off the track leading down to the main road are two grand late-Victorian mansion houses. **Edgehill**, *c.*1870, gothicised with parapeted bay windows, decorated ridge line and wrought-iron ornamentation over the door. **Lynwood**, at the end of L'Estrange Terrace, of similar age and style, no less grand, but more secluded. **Gowanlea**, *c.*1880, corner terraced cottage, with tiny spire over left bay window and exquisite painted glass in the windows' upper sashes. Remnants of **Bridge Mill** at the corner house.

By the 1790s, the Hillfoots villages used the combination of hills for sheep grazing, steep burns for water power and the proximity of a huge market in the central belt to create a very early concentration of industrial revolution activity. It became a major woollen manufacturing district. Alva had the most weavers (67 as compared with Tillicoultry's 21) producing handwoven cloth, or serge, and blankets from cottage-based looms. The first Alva woollen mills were built *c.*1800 and, from 1815, water was used to power the spinning machinery. By 1830 Alva had nine water-powered spinning mills, although the vast bulk of the wool was by now imported.

In the 1820s the local landowner, James Johnstone, keen to help develop the industry, opened up Alva Glen as a source of water power by blasting away rock faces and constructing a dam from which water was conveyed to the mills along wooden troughs or lades. The water power was gradually supplemented by, then superseded by, coal-fired steam power in the latter half of the 19th century. According to Charles Roger in 1853, *Alva was wont to be famed for the manufacture of serges; the staple trade now consists in the production of plaidings and blanketings. There are also very extensive factories for the manufacture of tartan shawls and chequered cassimeres.* The woollen mills then developed in other areas of the town, notable examples being the Glentana works and the brick-built mills around Henry Street.

Above *Cochrane Cairn.* Right *Cairn and hall, The Cochranes.*

The Cochrane Foundation administers the 1942 bequest of three brothers Cochrane – James, Charles and John – whose parents emigrated to Albany, New York State, in the 1860s. The family prospered, originally through manufacturing shawls, an art presumably learnt in Alva. The brothers, latterly of Philadelphia, made numerous gifts to Alva, especially the Cochrane Park and Hall. John Cochrane was named after his uncle, Dr John Eadie.

Old Town c.1920.

About 1700 the then Laird of Alva, Sir John Erskine, decided to lay out a village in the form of a square; that became Green Square (although only the north and west sides were built at first), located immediately behind the present Johnstone Arms Hotel. The area around Alva Green was feued for housing by weavers (predominantly), labourers and craftsmen, during the 18th century and the pattern was continued by the new Johnstone lairds of the 19th century. In 1770–6, the Erskines feued out the south side of the old road, their plan being to extend the village north of Green Square by granting simple feus to anyone prepared to build. Duke Street (or Middle Row) had only to be sufficiently wide *sae that a horse and a sack of meal on his back could pass,* and the feu duty could be paid in *kain hens good and sufficient, or fit for the spit when delivered.* It was claimed to be the narrowest named street in Scotland.

The Cochranes, 1947–50, James Shearer
Pretty series of cottages and taller blocks built as retirement homes by the Cochrane Foundation, in well-detailed stonework with pantiled hipped roofs and the **Boll Bell**.

West of the Burn
Upper **Brook Street**, formerly Boll Lane, was the centre for the water-powered woollen mills, and many old foundations still visible. Brick-built engineering works, also now Stephen Clark Fabrications, at head of Brook Street, grafted onto 1829 Alva village jail. Stump of what may be an ashlar-based chimney remains built into the steeply banked corner opposite the Island.

Former handloom weaving sheds and weavers' cottages survive in **Erskine Street**. **No 5 Inn**, once in Bridge Place, *c.*1900, on site of William Whyt's 1692 brewhouse, *where Robert Burns rested for refreshment in 1787,* states the plaque *erected by Alva Burns Club 1899*; modernised beyond recognition. Dominating the end of Erskine

Street, but really bounded by Queen Street and Park Street, is **Alva Academy**, 1967–9, County Architect: one-, two- and three-storey, flat-roofed blocks of that period brought to a climax by monstrous concrete-frame water tower. Entrance
82 court presided over by **swimming pool and leisure centre**, 1980, Central Regional Council Architects; bold concrete buttressing frames a building remarkable for its utilisation of solar energy in this northern climate. This replaced Alva's Victorian public swimming baths and wash houses, at the end of Park Street, which closed late 1970s. A 1995 plaque commemorates the original gift of both the baths, opened 1874, and the adjacent **Johnstone Park**, in or around 1836, to the people of Alva by James Johnstone of Alva House. **77 Park Street**, *c.*1860, now a house, was offices of former army drill hall at corner of Copland Place, still used by Alva Detachment Army Cadet Force; a delight of arched windows, rounded dormers and brick-detailed Dutch gable to front.

Beauclerc Street, feued by James Johnstone from 1796 and originally Back Raw, it was renamed after Johnstone's daughter, Lady Jemima Beauclerc. Running westwards from the burn, the street is formed of groups of little cottages, some
83 with dormer windows and porches. **Barnaigh**, 1860s' mansion barely visible through tall trees and shrubs of large terraced garden at foot of Carnaughton Glen, a splendid example of high-Victorian eclecticism: grand Italianate tower to south east with mock canon gargoyles sparring with tall, piended French château roof. Rainwater heads bearded with angelic wings above twisted downpipes. It belonged to the Wilsons of Glentana Mill. **Listerlea**, 1873, substantial gothicised villa, now within Cochrane Park, built as manse for United Presbyterian (now Alva Parish) Church.

Top *Swimming pool and leisure centre, Alva Academy.* Middle *War memorial, Johnstone Park and old swimming pool.* Above *77 Park Street.*

As **Back Road**, the old road continues westwards, now hosting a series of individual modern villas and chalets, each identified by an ostentatious name. Resounding **Jinglebank**, timber and stone clad, **Balbaird**, a dark brick pavilion.

Barnaigh.

Expansion to the South
Arrival of the new Hillfoots main road in 1806 pulled Alva south from Green Square to the new Stirling Street. The lairds were quick to seize the opportunity of raising capital and James Johnstone offered the first feus in the same year. Resulting buildings usually simple,

Top and above *The Boll before and after restoration.*

The Johnstones of Alva

Aged 16, John Johnstone, 1734–95, fifth son of a Lanarkshire laird, went to Calcutta as an artillery officer and, in 1757, *aided much to the success of the battle of Plassey,* under Robert Clive, although he later joined the *storm of obloquey* against Clive in the 1770s. He prudently waited until after Clive's suicide in 1774 before spending the vast fortune he *earnt* in India. In 1778 he added Alva to his Selkirk and Dumfriesshire estates, and yet in 1788 still remained *immensely rich* with a fortune of £300,000. His son, James Raymond Johnstone, 1768–1830, had 16 children, of which the eldest, James, 1801–88, took Sarah Mary L'Estrange as his second wife in 1862 *against strong competition in Brussels from a foreign royal prince.*

Alva Primary School.

undecorated Scots Georgian houses, unified by almost identical Doric pilastered doorway which occurs, less frequently, in similarly aged houses throughout Alva and Tillicoultry. Streets of millworkers' cottages named after the Johnstone family were laid out during late 19th century south of the main road. Most redeveloped for housing by local authorities during 1960s and '70s. Old **railway station** in George Street opposite Lower Queen Street, which ended the 1863 line from Alloa by Cambus, converted to house. Alva railway branch was prevented from joining the east-going line at Tillicoultry by James Johnstone who forbade it pass through his Alva estate. **Brook Street** is the direct road into Alva from Alloa, south entry marked by **The Boll**, neat gothicised farmhouse, *c.*1850, renovated and significantly extended, 2000, Colin Machin, following a period of dereliction. Farmhouse provides vast single entertaining space and new west wing has fabulous views of the Ochils and the carse to the Wallace Monument. Behind, courtyard of four new red-roofed holiday-let cottages on the site of the farm steadings.

Alva Primary School, 1976,
Central Regional Council Architects
Friendly single-storey hall with classroom courtyard, and enclosed bridge over Alva Burn leading to two-storey block of more senior classrooms, in crisp rectangular blocks of dark brickwork, on the site of Meadow Mill. Link with the past formed by retention of the ancient school bell as a feature within entrance foyer.

In **Henry Street**, a number of 19th-century textile mills were built in the locality of the burn. Burnbrae Works and Greenfield Mill have gone; and after close inspection all that remains are the
85 small rubble-built 1830 **Handloom Weaving Mill**, at northern corner with Brook Street, and, under heavy brown dry-dash, parts of **Burnside Works**, 1870s' polychromatic brick woollen mill, both converted to and much interspaced with new housing.

Greenhead, series of good two-storey solid Thirties' blocks; flat roofs now pitched, exposed brick dry-dash rendered and windows all changed – with resultant loss of all character. **Minto Gardens** blocks adjacent, 1919, have only lost their original windows; a pioneering example of Addison Act houses by William Kerr for Alva Burgh Council: but in appearance conventional, two-storey blocks.

Dr John Eadie, 1810–76, distinguished theological professor in Glasgow, was the son of an Alva road-mender. Well known in the United Presbyterian church, Eadie became a supporter of Biblical Criticism and a contributor to the publication in 1881 of the Revised Version of the English Bible.

Left *Cochrane Hall.* Below *Scotland's Mill Trail Visitor Centre.*

Stirling Street
Cochrane Hall, West Stirling Street, 1929, William Kerr (colour p.75)
Cross between South African and Home Counties vernacular, completely out of character with the Hillfoots architecture whose verticality is acknowledged in its dramatic steep roof – the dominant feature – hipped to the sides rising into half gables, extending over little hipped wings to the front at either side and rising over huge curved, gabled projecting porch . Wooden columns form a veranda between porch and wings. Upgraded early 1990s.

86 **Scotland's Mill Trail Visitor Centre**, Glentana Mills, West Stirling Street, 1874 A 15-window powerloom shed fronts the main road, well detailed in two-tone brick, with attractive corbelled cornice and recessed

Right *Scotland's Mill Trail Visitor Centre.*
Top and above *Dalmore Centre.*

Below *Hillfoots Picture Palace Theatre.*
Bottom *Alva Parish Church.* Right *115 &
117 Stirling Street.*

windows. May have been designed by Glasgow architect Robert Baldie in 1887, with old smithy and engine house behind; converted 1994, Clackmannan District Council Architects. Now information point for the Mill Trail, with steel-columned entrances, gift and fashion shops, coffee shop and exhibition telling the story of the textile industry (colour p.75).

Dalmore Centre, *c.*1870, is the gothic Dalmore School providing a community centre. Cast-iron griffin rainwater hoppers and bellcote finial are a delight. **Hillfoots Picture Palace Theatre**, 1921, symmetrical brick façade with gable oculi, had a balcony and could seat nearly 1,000; long since converted to meat-processing factory. Former **Free Church**, opposite, retains its frontage, converted to housing behind.

87 **Alva Parish Church**, 1842, possibly John Melvin Built by United Secession congregation of 1838, becoming United Presbyterian in 1847, United Free in 1900 and from 1929 the Eadie Church of Scotland. Suitably forbidding with its mixture of gothic pinnacles, arches and castellations. In 1984 it replaced St Serf's (see p.95) as the parish church. Adjoining house, **Peaches Nursery**, is of the original new road feuing. Further east, **115 & 117 Stirling Street**, 1995, Bracewell Stirling Architects

for Ochil View Housing Association end terrace block addition, echoing the proportions of the old, in white render with corner date stone. Pleasant courtyard to rear. Alva Co-operative Bazaar Society, was founded in 1845, and grew in strength, represented by buildings on both sides of Stirling Street, dating from 1888 (**Co-op Late Shop**, on north side) and with the 1895 jubilee clock (now **ET's Bakery** and **The Orchard**) on older south side building (colour p.75). **Alva Glen Hotel**, 1807, which now continues to Brook Street, was built as the Blue Bell Tavern to serve the first travellers on the new road, its much later finely sculpted ornamentation at cornice level and around the door gently copied for its east extension – now obscured by terracotta paintwork of **Manzil Restaurant**.

Opposite, **Johnstone Arms Hotel**, 18th century, remodelled c.1840 to provide two-storey three-bay frontage, with larger complex of 19th-century buildings behind; modern conservatory extension. **St John Vianney's RC Church**, 1925, symmetrical gothic frontage with arched windows either side of the door, round window above and half-timber detailing to gable apex. Adjacent **presbytery**, a little Victorian gothic cottage with Dutch-gabled porch.

Top *Johnstone Arms Hotel.* Above *St John Vianney's RC Church and presbytery.*

Eastern approach
Contains a number of textile mills, old and new. Part of the yard at **Brookfield** contains relics of Ross 1865 spinning mills. Hodgson's (formerly Archibald's) **Ochilvale Mills**, built at end of 19th century, main block being of red and white brick; **Mill Shop** created from rubble-built wool store. **Berryfield** is the 1974 Coblecrook Dyeworks (relocated from the west of Alva), dominated by tall steel chimney and occupied by Hodgsons and the Tullis plastics factory from Tullibody Tannery (plus the tiny Berryfield Mill Shop). Behind is **Kelpie E-M**, 1999, Harley and Murray, rather good small building for a computer company, turquoise clad, with buttressed dark masonry, glass frontage and white circular tower. The most interesting looking new business unit in Clackmannanshire.

Below *Ochilvale Mills.* Left *Kelpie E-M.*

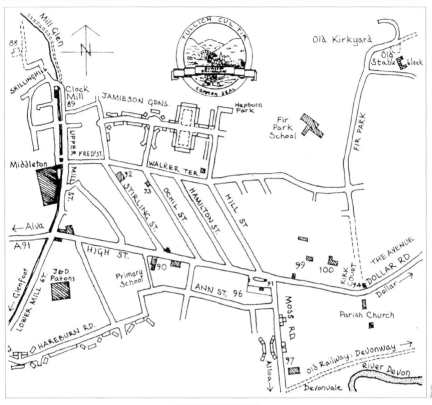

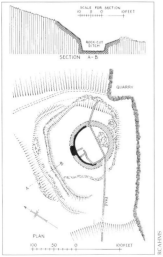

Survey drawings of motte-and-bailey castle excavated at Castle Craig.

TILLICOULTRY

Like other Hillfoots communities, modern Tillicoultry owes its existence to the fast-running burns tumbling down the Ochils to join the River Devon. To appreciate its real character, visitors have to leave the wide main road and penetrate uphill. It developed from the small village of Westerton at the upper part of Tillicoultry Burn, by Clock Mill, where the old Stirling High Road passed over Middleton Bridge and cut along what is now Frederick Street. An ancient fortress is known to have existed on **Castle Craig** above, perpetuated in the names of the early 19th-century textile mills. The parish was formed by three villages: Westerton, Coalsnaughton on the ridge to the south, and Easterton (or Earlstown), which no longer exists, near Harviestoun.

In 1803, William Chalmers noted *that this parish has been for some hundred years famous for a species of manufacture, called Tillicoultry serge, a kind of shalloon, having worsted warp and linen woof* (weft). Eight woollen mills were established by the Tillicoultry Burn of which only **Clock Mill**, 1824, and **J & D Paton's Mill**, from 1825, survive.

88 Foundations of **Craigfoot Mill**, 1808 and 1838, still visible below Tillicoultry Quarry, which has been gouging aggregate and dressed stone from the Ochils since 1880. This and other mills were powered by water brought along a timber lade and aqueduct from the 1824 dam in Mill Glen. Another timber dam, higher up the burn, now ruined, used to conserve water flow overnight. The massive iron waterwheel at Craigfoot was 30ft in diameter.

Mill Glen, 1926, Arthur Bracewell
Spectacular walk of bridges, paths and steps engineered by Bracewell provide a route amid rare plants and wildlife into the rolling Ochils. First bridge is a fine stone arch with plaque commemorating the Glen opening. Nature trail created within the Glen, where the remains of the timber **dam** can be seen.

Above *Remains of the dam, Mill Glen.*
Left *Clock Mill.*

Upper Mill Street
Clock Mill, 1824
Built by James and George Walker from Galashiels to manufacture blankets, plaids and tartan shawls, its gable, with clock and ball finial, faces downhill. Mill was powered both from the lade and by an engine house (now gone) driven by underground shafts. Now Tillicoultry Business Centre. Only rubble perimeter walls alongside the burn remain of **Middleton Mills**, 1836 complex of rubble buildings by Robert Archibald and Sons, when they moved from the 1805 Middleton Mill, later incorporated. From 1934 used as Samuel Jones subsidiary, the Dunedin Stationery Company. Fragments of entrance offices, 1926, Arthur Bracewell, also survive.

Doorway, Middleton Mills.

Shillinghill
Off Upper Mill Street, attractive stone-laced, white-rendered houses, 1957–8, A G Bracewell, for the burgh council in a conscious attempt to retain

Shillinghill.

Tillicoultry was an early centre of
Hillfoots textiles, its first mill
established in the 1790s. Between 1801
and 1851 the population of Tillicoultry
increased from 916 to 4,686, an
expansion responsible for much of the
current architectural character of the
town. It remained an important
manufacturing centre after being
overtaken in importance by Alloa in
mid-century. The first mills were built
next to the burn for water power, but
were superseded by steam powered
mills in the 1830s. As the upper
environs of the burns were already
occupied, new sites were found lower
down the burn and to the south east of
the town. Devonside was established as
a village to accommodate the new influx
on the south bank of the Devon, steam-
powered mills being in operation there
by the 1830s. The high peak of textile
manufacturing was reached around
1900, since when it has declined, here, to
virtual extinction.

Below *The Woolpack.* Middle *Former
J & D Paton's Mill office block.* Bottom
High Street.

some of the historic flavour of the Old Town.
Nearby gardens by the burn, 1970, formed from a
bequest from Tillicoultry's longest serving town
councillor, William Jamieson. A variety of old
cottages, mostly early 19th century, in Glassford
Square, Cairnton Place, Frederick Street and
Crofthead. **The Woolpack**, old weavers' inn,
charming little two-storey hostelry within the
clustered cottages of **Glassford Square**, redolent
of the days when wool was brought across the
Ochils from Blackford by pack horse. Glassford
Square can be dated from Duncan Glassford's
short ownership of the Tillicoultry estate: 1806–10.

Former J & D Paton's Mill, Lower Mill Street, 1836
Enormously long, 34-window, low rubble mill is
part of what was once the most productive textile
mill in Scotland, that of James and David Paton
of Alloa. The gold medal which they won in the
Great Exhibition in 1851 symbolised the
international reputation of their shawls, tartans
and tweeds. In the 20th century Paton's produced
tartans and serges, notably for military use
during the First World War. Mill and three-storey
office block converted to flats from 1991, with
new-build housing for Ochil View Housing
Association to the north (colour p.76).

High Street
Principal businesses emigrated south to the new
highway after it was built in 1806. Tillicoultry
enjoyed few grand houses, as there were only a
handful of mill owning families, and textile mills
were Tillicoultry's only industry until the 1920s.
Consequently, majority of buildings in High
Street were purely utilitarian commercial
premises, with little notion of architectural
quality. Many replaced, late 1960s, by widely
spaced three-storey housing.

Tillicoultry's early 19th-century hotels were all
clustered together to serve custom on the new
road: **Royal Arms** (formerly Hotel) and former

Crown Hotel on north side of High Street, and Castle Craig Hotel opposite. All two storey, with plain margins and Doric doors. Crown Hotel now flatted as Primrose Court, displaying thick plastic windows and infill doors. Granite fountain on the bridge gifted by Provost Walker on his retirement in 1900.

Tillicoultry Library, High Street, c.1830
Formed from group of three imposing Georgian houses, pink harled, with painted margins and quoins. Easternmost part has fluted Doric-columned porch; some windows altered. Elegant, 90 classically rectangular, 1840 West Church converted, 1982, by Alex Strang Associates to sheltered housing. Upper parts of windows graced with reflective glass to conceal lowered ceilings within.

Tillicoultry Library.

In August 1877 *one of the most calamitous floods took place among the front of the Ochil range that was ever known to man … after a deluging rain had continued for some time … Tillicoultry Burn came raging down in one almighty wall of water of some seven or eight feet high, carrying everything before it …* The flood swept away large sections of Upper Mill Street – houses, bridges and the Castle Mill – and tragically drowned the mill owner and a mill hand.

Left *Murray Square c.1950.* Below *Clock, Murray Square.*

91 Murray Square, from 1930
One of the first bus stations in Scotland, instigated by Provost Thomas Murray who was worried about accidents occurring from the eight bus services (334 buses daily) which used Tillicoultry as a terminus at that time. Murray gifted the prefabricated clock, 1931, rose and rock gardens and The Thomas Murray Howff for Aged Men, 1936, a little octagonal reading room, sadly demolished 2001 (fireplace, ceramic plaques and lintel all salvaged by the council's museum). Excepting the clock, buildings were by Arthur Bracewell, most interesting being the bus shelter (also demolished). The square should be restored.

The Village Expansion – Weavers' Cottages
From the 1840s a wealthier class of mill worker appeared in Tillicoultry able to buy or rent a small cottage, and new streets were built at an oblique angle north of High Street.

Top *Stirling Street*. Above *52 Stirling Street.*

Ben Cleuch, the highest Ochil Peak (2,363ft), was to have a railway to its summit. The line was surveyed in 1863 in the hope that *the scheme will be carried through as it will bring our beautiful Ochils more into notice … and attract crowds of tourists to our really picturesque neighbourhood.* Fortunately for the *beautiful Ochils* this was one engineering proposition the Victorians abandoned.

Right *Tower, Ochil Street*. Below *1920 housing block, Hill Street.* Bottom *2 Walker Terrace.*

Stirling Street has single and double cottages to the west with canted attic dormers. The east (or sunny) side has grander houses and cottages. 92 **No 52**, Daiglen Kiltmakers (former Walker Institute), *c.*1850, gothicised house, extended 1919, by William Kerr in neat renaissance style.

93 **Tower**, Ochil Street, 1879, John Melvin Competition-winning Victorian curiosity, donated by mill owner James Archibald, as campanile to 1859 Town Hall (demolished 1986). Square at lower stages, rising to balcony decorated by four tiny turrets, tower continues as louvred octagon to four-faced clock and parapet, originally surmounted by cupola. **Ochil Street**, from 1850s, perhaps finest of the Tillicoultry planned weavers' streets: stone cottages with regular slate roofs, each with neat front garden. Plainer, later cottages of **Hamilton Street** forgo their front gardens and were also developed by Ochil United House Building Society. An 1879 fountain commemorates the Co-operative Baking Society's jubilee.

Hill Street, late 19th century
Mixture of cottages and houses some with front gardens, and some with minor ornament. Two of the first **housing blocks** in Tillicoultry designed by William Kerr following the 1919 Addison Act on the east side.

Walker Terrace, late 19th century
Row of larger Victorian villas with gothic elements along old Hillfoots high road. **No 38**, 1889, Adam Frame, originally manse but now offices of Bracewell Stirling Architects, fine gothic villa, with decorated ridge, front gable and bay window.

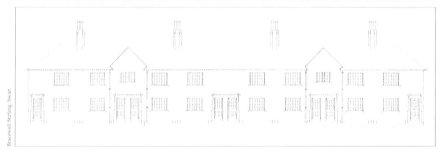

Bracewell Setting-Swan

Jamieson Gardens, 1931–9, Arthur Bracewell
Unremarkable individually, although decorative
door mouldings are a particular delight, the real
value of this five-phase housing development is
its Garden City layout (colour p.76). **Scheme No
1**, 1931, seven blocks at the half crescented
junction of Cairnton Place. **Scheme No 2**, 1932,
continues eastwards, two blocks of houses on
each side of the road, with pedimented gables
above entrances. **Scheme No 3**, 1933, forms
crescent opposite Ochilview Road, distinguished
by projecting door lintels. **Scheme No 5**, 1939,
superseding an unbuilt scheme, completed the
Arthur Bracewell part of Jamieson Gardens and
Ochilview Road. East/west road continued
through dramatic rectangle. To north and south,
wide grassed areas with long terraces of brick
housing. Last three blocks were 1941 amendment,
war shortages compelling concrete-beam floors,
flat roofs and concrete stairs in place of pitched
roofs and floors of timber construction.

Fir Park School, 1966, W H Henry
Composition of rectangular, single-storey brick
boxes enfolding a four-storey one, now annexe to
Alva Academy which provides secondary
education for all Hillfoots towns, Fir Park
presently accommodating first year. Dry ski
slope, 1985, provides useful (if unsightly) facility.
Fir Park Estate, 1967–8, A G Bracewell, private
housing meandering up steep hillside towards
old kirkyard; simple bungalows to the east,
Alpine, flat-roofed chalets to the west, stepped
down for the gradient.

Old Kirkyard, medieval onwards
Site of parish church from 11th century to 1773,
well worth the steep climb, kirkyard contains
some important stones, including 12th-century
hog-backed stone with ridge down the centre and
1522 baker's stone. All in fragile condition,
vulnerable to vandalism and require attention to
ensure survival.

Top *Scheme No2, Jamieson Gardens.*
Above *Jamieson Gardens.*

Below *Fir Park School.* Bottom *1723
headstone in the Old Kirkyard, with the
ploughshare, colter and harrow of the
ploughman.*

Right *Tillicoultry House.* Top *Stable block.*
Middle *Lodge.* Above *Harviestoun
Country Inn.*

Below *Collier's Court.* Middle *Last 1920s'
house in Ann Street by William Kerr to
retain original features.* Bottom *Triple villa,
Moss Road.*

Tillicoultry House, 1829 (demolished)
Good classical house, de-roofed after the last laird
quit the district, 1938, demolished *c*.1960. All that
remains is tall retaining wall of garden and fine
classical **stable block** (converted to flats). West
front arched, flanked by blank archways and
topped with splendid cupola. Horses had the
94 better bargain. **Lodge**, Dollar Road, early 19th
century, possibly William Stirling, has overscaled
pedimented doorway facing parish church.

95 **Harviestoun Country Inn** (former Tillicoultry
Mains), 1837–8, William Stirling
Delightful Georgian three-sided steading, east
and west ranges single storey, ending in higher
pavilions. North range has arched cartsheds with
grain lofts above. Sympathetically converted to
restaurant, 1990, Colin Machin. Civic Trust
Commendation, 1993 (see p.5).

South of the Main Road
96 **Collier's Court**, 1984, Clackmannan District
Council Architects, provides excellent courtyard
of self-professed East Neuk vernacular,
surrounding harbour of children's play
equipment. **Stoneyacre**, 1932–4, Arthur
Bracewell, has Garden City housing blocks,
similar to Jamieson Gardens. **Hareburn Road**
houses nearest Lower Mill Street are excellent
examples of formal blocks, with great central
entrances approached by long pathways.

Moss Road, from 1934, Arthur Bracewell
Designed to the requirements of Sidney Platfoot
of Devonvale, houses display fine sense of social
status in their variety – some management and
some workers. **36-46 Moss Road**, 1935, three
double villas with parapeted curved bay
windows to each side. **52-62 Moss Road**, 1937,
two unique triple villas, with distinguishing
1930s' curved bays. Bracewell designed

Devonvale Crescent in 1939, built 1946–53, as two back-to-back crescents of houses forming built realisation of the butterfly, the Samuel Jones symbol. **Recreation Ground**, acquired by Platfoot in 1925 to safeguard future expansion, used in the meantime for football, cricket pitches, a bowling green and tennis courts – each with its elegant **pavilion**. Bowling facilities alone survive. The 1964 **West Mill** was the expected expansion, by Arthur Bracewell's son, A G Bracewell, now replaced by **Sterling Mills Designer Retail Village**, 1998, Lyons, Sleeman and Hoare, with Dalziel Design Partnership (colour p.76). Simple blockwork buildings arranged as streets of discount shops facing into each other, in the form of long gabled ranges stopped by square pavilion end blocks. Good metal silhouettes gates at each entrance illustrate mills and factories. **Devonvale War Memorial**, C d'O Pilkington Jackson, is Platfoot's tribute to his workers who fell during the Second World War; now forms entrance gates to the 97 'village'. **Devonvale Hall**, 1940, Arthur Bracewell, displays the company's Camberwell Beauty butterfly above and traces of modernism round the entrance. Upgraded early 1990s (colour p.76).

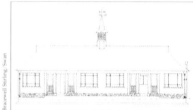

Top *1948 tennis pavilion, survived by its sister bowling pavilion.* Middle *Sterling Mills Designer Retail Village and Sterling Warehouse.* Above *Devonvale Hall.* Left *Devonvale Mill, c.1880.*

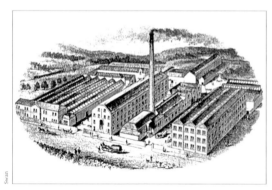

98 **Sterling Warehouse**, Moss Road, from 1846 Large three-storey, six-by-sixteen window, white-painted stone, with associated buildings of 1860s. Established by J & R Archibald as **Devonvale Mill**, it concentrated on tweed manufacture for which it became famous. Used as army barracks during the First World War, ground floor providing stabling for 800 horses, and purchased, 1920, by Samuel Jones of Camberwell for a papercoating plant. Mill buildings now used as showrooms by thriving furniture retail company. **Butterfly Inn**, 1954, A G Bracewell, converted from works canteen and traps a ceramic butterfly on its gable.

I think that for beauty, our southern style of building with its plentiful supply of windows, white enamelling, rustic arches and red roofs, takes a lot of beating, though naturally Scots houses are of necessity built for strength and warmth. Thus wrote Sidney Platfoot (d.1963), two years after moving to Tillicoultry from Camberwell in 1923, as managing director of a new paper-coating firm, Samuel Jones and Co. (Devonvale) Ltd. Recognising the value of a contented workforce, Platfoot set about establishing facilities for its benefit. He employed the talents of a Lethaby-trained architect, **Arthur Bracewell**, 1891–1953, who had been brought north to Tillicoultry in 1925 by the Salts of Saltaire, then owners of Middleton and Devonpark Mills, to renovate and design minor extensions. Platfoot's repeated motto, in product and building alike, was *Devonvale means quality.*

Top *Westbourne*. Right *Beechwood*.
Middle *Ceiling of principal first-floor room, Beechwood*. Above *Kirk Court*.

A surveyor's plan of **Beechwood** of 1911 shows that the house originally had larger, intensively planned grounds with stables, a kitchen garden (with access lane to the east), a (bowling?) green, tennis courts, curling rink, swimming pond (which was covered in the 1930s), vineries, a conservatory (replaced by the kitchen), as well as extensive shrubberies and gardens. Now divided into three with housing in the rear grounds.

St Serf's Parish Church.

Dollar Road

99 **Westbourne**, 1868, probably John Melvin
Small but grand gothic Scots house with castellated bay windows, whose gatelodge gives over-opulent effect. Stables converted by
100 A G Bracewell to his own house. **Beechwood**, 1860–70, Adam Frame, largest house in Tillicoultry, originally asymmetrical gothic with square bay to the west. Large extension to west and north doubled the house. Exceptional gothic plasterwork inside (colour p.76). **Kirk Court**, 1985, Duncan Stirling, three-sided courtyard of staggered, terraced brick sheltered houses. **The Avenue**, 1984, Duncan Stirling, continues the Kirk Court aesthetic, one-person houses using miners' row idiom, and the hill to stagger the roofline: formal entrances, pathways and gardens to north and large sunny private drying green to south.

St Serf's Parish Church, Dollar Road, 1827–9, William Stirling
Replacing, and possibly re-using elements of, 1773 church in neo-perpendicular gothic, impressive features are large octagonal bellcote to north end and buttressing to sides of each bay which continue into pointed finials, high above. Stained-glass window by Douglas Strachan. **Manse** from 1811.

Dollar Road Bungalows, 1933–51, Arthur Bracewell
Nine private bungalows by Devonvale Contractors (a subsidiary of Samuel Jones), the last one **Broomhall** (No 44), 1940, for Horace Platfoot, director and son of Devonvale Mill managing director. Butterfly-form plan.

Devonside, from 1834
Small village on southern bank of River Devon formed when first carding and spinning mill established downhill from Tillicoultry. Within

two years, five factories were carding, spinning, weaving and dyeing on the site; with Devonvale Mill across the Devon. Some later amalgamated into **Devonpark Mill**.

COALSNAUGHTON

Third village of Tillicoultry parish, high on south ridge above the valley, reached by steep and winding road from Devonside. Its name derived from *Collie Nechtan* – the wood of Nechtan – possibly after the Pictish King Nechtan Macderile. Until 1950s, village core consisted of Ramsay Street, with small cottages, many whitewashed and pantiled (one had *RDED 1683* over its lintel), and 19th-century miners' rows by Robert Bald, the enlightened Alloa mining engineer.

Top *Dollar Road bungalow.* Middle *Ramsay Street, Coalsnaughton, before redevelopment in the 1950s.* Above *Coalsnaughton Public Hall and Library.* Left *Tillicoultry from Coalsnaughton Brae.*

101 Coalsnaughton Public Hall and **Library**, 1907, John S Leishman, extended 1925, William Kerr Low pink-harled, rambling complex of slate-roofed community buildings, doorways well marked with relevant titles, and Tudor-like gabled parapets. Kerr's lesser hall has typical square bay windows with overhanging hipped eaves. Upgraded 1999.

Aberdona House, from 18th century
Set in extensive grounds east of Gartmorn Dam, enchanting group with early 18th-century wing to north and mid-18th-century wing to east, joined *c.*1860 at south-west angle by tall three-storey Tudor tower complete with battlements. Retains many 18th-century fittings. Built by the Erskines of Alva, and became part of Harviestoun Estate (now the principal residence) in 1860 – the battlemented tower being similar to that added when Sir Andrew Orr bought Harviestoun the previous year.

Aberdona House.

Harviestoun Castle.

John Tait, 1727–1800, a wealthy Edinburgh lawyer, had bought *a tolerably good house* on the old Harviestoun road in 1780. His son Craufurd, 1765–1832, was the principal mover in the matter of the new Turnpike Road from Stirling to Kinross, from 1806. The latter improved both house and estate, demolishing the original hamlets on the road, and from 1804 reconstructed much of Harviestoun Castle, with its battlements and corner towers. The stretch of the new Turnpike at Harviestoun was designed with curves following the River Devon to provide changing views through the valley. In 1802 he created a beautiful garden around the mansion using, according to his daughter Lady Wake, Milton's description of the Garden of Eden as his guide. It had wild water and formal gardens and a burn running through a cave (still there and incorporating a 1688 date stone) descending over a small waterfall to a pool. Tait introduced agricultural and mechanical innovations to the estate, examples being a mechanical spit in the kitchen, powered by water from the Harviestoun Burn, and a three-tiered poultry house for hens on the top, turkeys in the middle and ducks and geese on the bottom, with interconnecting ladders. He experimented too much with steam engines for his coal mines, which soon led to his interdiction and subsequent bankruptcy.

RCAHMS

Harviestoun Castle, 1804 (on older site), tower 1859 (demolished)
Blown up 1970; now commemorated by 1859 gatelodges, stables and the home farm.

Stable block, late 18th century, U-shaped plan, fronted by long, classical ashlar block; pediment above arched pend at centre. Extensive **home farm**, *c.*1820, comprises two-storey E-plan steading with cart-arches, crowsteps and classical mouldings, dominated by fine octagonal tower with stone spire. Small, but grand farmhouse at either side of steading, each with elegant pyramidal roof topped by endearing group of four central chimneys. **East** and **West Lodges**, 1859, are tiny battlemented versions of the castle; small commemorative cairn to Robert Burns at East Lodge. A private coal mine operated within the estate until 1989. **Tait's Tomb**, small burial ground of the Taits of Harviestoun (see p.88), within high semicircular stone wall at sharp bend in main road.

Below *Home farm, Harviestoun Castle.* Bottom *Sheardale House from John Millar's biography.*

Swan

Clackmannanshire Council

Sheardale House, *c.*1855 (demolished *c.*1973)
Built on north face of Sheardale Ridge for John Millar – who must have acquired the estate from the Harviestoun trustees – large two-storey house with French-style mansards, suitable for generous entertaining. Interested in garden design, for the house had lavish terraces decorated with cement statues, vases and lions, Millar was one of Edinburgh's leading china and glass merchants and was responsible for the life-sized fireclay statues of Victoria and Albert, now in the Museum 102 of Scotland. **Wester Sheardale**, 18th century, was the original estate house closer to the river, whose site dates from at least 1605. L-shaped steading, with outside stair to lofts above arched carriage doorway, heraldic panel and large walled kitchen garden behind. **Sheardale village**, attractive 18th- and 19th-century slated or pantiled cottages lining Sheardale Road.

DOLLAR
Castle Campbell, 15th century onward
Set high above Dollar on natural eminence, guarded by steep ravines on three sides, Castle Campbell was the chief lowland seat of the Earls of Argyll. Tower, dating from 15th century, is the oldest and best-preserved section. Two lower chambers in mid-16th-century east range retain unusual vaults with moulded ribs, similar to those of the top room of the tower which have odd grotesque masks. Fronting the east range is a remarkable palace-like screen, with two-bay loggia to courtyard, and small paired windows and stringcourses forming little galleries above, a significant renaissance composition added *c.*1594, along with six-storey staircase against the tower and much shorter square one against the south range, may be by William Schaw of Sauchie. South range of state apartments dates from *c.*1500, with large fireplace, and south-facing

Castle Campbell in 1797 by Francis Grose from the MacGibbon and Ross Collection.

An 1823 advertisement for *The Lordship and Estate of Campbell and the Estates of Harviestoun, Sheardale, Mains of Dollar and Lawhill, together with the Patronage of the Parish of Dollar and extensive Seams of Coal and other Minerals* states that *The Mansion-house of Harviestoun is beautifully situated, surrounded by thriving woods and plantations, and is large and commodious, and in every way suitable to the estate. The Stables and Coach-houses are large and convenient; and there are also excellent farm offices on an extensive scale. The garden and shrubbery are considered to be laid out with great taste. The Ruins of Castle Campbell, so much celebrated by Pennant, and other tourists, are situated in the eastern part of the estate.* The estate was not sold until Sir Andrew Orr bought it in 1859.

Colin Campbell, 1st Earl of Argyll, acquired the castle (then known as Gloume) through his wife, an heiress of Walter Stewart of Lorne. During the centuries when the range of buildings around the tower were constructed, the Earls of Argyll held some of the highest positions in the land – ambassadors, Masters of the King's Household, Justiciar of Scotland, Lord High Chancellor of Scotland – and later were the strong and constant supporters of the Protestant faith. It is likely that John Knox administered the Holy Sacrament for one of the first times during his visit to the castle in 1556.

Craiginnan Home Farm was where John Christie, *the literary shepherd*, was born in October 1712 and lived until 1793. He amassed a library of 370 volumes, *all neatly bound and lettered on the back, and with a bookmark and printed bookplate in each one.*

Left *Castle Campbell.* Below *Plan of courtyard level.*

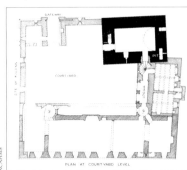

PLAN AT COURTYARD LEVEL

windows, above a row of cellars, with gallery behind overlooking courtyard and stump of octagonal stairtower to the west.

Castle ceased to be important round mid-17th century. It was supposed that General Monk destroyed it in 1654, but Argyll co-operated with Monk and it was rebel Royalists during the Earl of Glencairn's rising who burnt it. Monk wrote to Cromwell on 29 July 1654: *Some small parties of the enemy are abroad in the country, and on Monday and Tuesday last burn't Castle Campbell.* Argyll was executed on the restoration of Charles II. First repairs carried out by James Orr of Harviestoun when he succeeded his brother in 1874.

On a clear day, the view from the tower is one of the finest in Scotland; when cloudy, enclosed by rolling banks of mist, there is a sense of awe-inspiring isolation and timelessness (colour p.77). *Historic Scotland; open to the public; guidebook available*

Top *Billings' engraving of the top chambers of the tower, c.1850.* Middle *Conjectural restoration shows c.1594 east range with loggia and tall stairtower, but omits the continuation of the short square tower into the far right of the range (centre of drawing); the courtyard gallery and octagonal stairtower behind the south range are shown restored to the right of the drawing.* Above *Long Bridge and Kemp's Score, c.1900.*

A romanticised view of Castle Campbell and Dollar Burnside, published 1838.

Dollar Glen

An enchanting and exhilarating walk past deep gorges and high waterfalls amid abundant plant life growing on the wooded slopes. Some inappropriate additions and, sadly, the famous **Long Bridge** over the gorge has gone, and there is a new west bank path. Paths continue above the castle and have been owned and maintained by the National Trust for Scotland since 1953.

Old Town of Dollar

Although the first reference to Dollar parish is in the Dark Ages, it figures little in early history. Utterly burnt, 1645, as part of an attack on the Earl of Argyll and Castle Campbell. First visible remains of pre-Academy Dollar are the village formed round the burn and Argyll's grain mill at the head of Mill Green (created as public

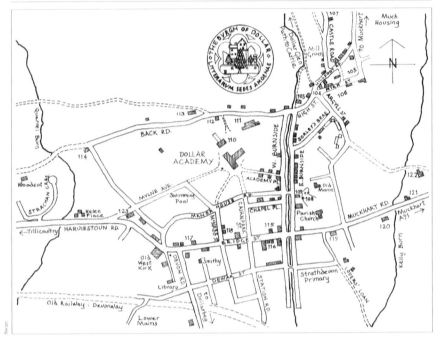

bleachfield by the Duke in the 18th century not long before Argyll sold the estate to Craufurd Tait of Harviestoun). In 1800 the first woollen mill was built, succeeded in 1822 by the harled stone

103 **Brunt Mill** at the North Bridge and foot of High Street, later preserved by Harviestoun Estate for *the amenity of Dollar* and, since 1991, converted to flats and providing a home for Dollar Museum, one of the most successful community museums in the country.

Brunt Mill by Jennifer Campbell.

Pre-Academy Dollar is now called the *Old Town,* east of North Bridge. Never a substantial community; so insignificant, indeed, that Robert Forsyth thought it merited no mention in 1804 in his *Beauties of Scotland.* William Chalmers, in 1803, called it *very small and mean.* Garnett, travelling through in 1798 from Dunfermline to Stirling, recorded *a small village with a wretched Inn. Although well situated for an Inn, it is unfortunate that there is not a house which would afford tolerable accommodation for travellers.*

Cross Keys House.

Cross Keys
The heart of the Old Town is the sloping square from which Argyll Street leads south, High Street to the east and west and Hillfoot Road to the north east. The name comes from the Cross Keys, a long-demolished pub. **Cross Keys House**, 1-3 Hillfoot Road, former 18th-century drovers' inn

From top: *2 & 4 High Street; Former village store and Priory; Southview; Moss Court, a blend of old and new.* Right *Baldinnes and The Luggy.*

Broomieknowe Cottage and Cashmere Cottage.

now converted to houses: wide, five-window house with crowstepped gables, **No 1** has rustic porch and basement (once a beer cellar) below. **No 3** restored, 1975, Duncan Stirling.

104   Former **village store**, High Street, 1806, now houses, was one of the grandest buildings in Dollar at the time of construction, with scrolled skewputts, architrave above door, well-proportioned windows and re-used 18th-century date stone. Emblem of horse rearing above the door is that of the Scottish Union Fire Insurance.

High Street

Upper section mainly lined with cottages of 1800–40 vintage, many feued, 1807, by the Duke of Argyll. Note quaint **Priory** with gabled dormer windows. Two houses behind, converted from garage workshop, previously a grainstore, started as original 1860 United Presbyterian Church, which moved to grander premises on Burnside in 1872. Pantiled, rubble-built cottages further up; **Southview** dated 1799, white harled, two storey to the rear and pantiled like its neighbour, No 34. Street-level entrance of **The Luggy**, easternmost house of **Baldinnes**, former farmhouse, conceals
105 former byre below. **Moss Court** and **Brewlands**
106 **Court**, 1970s Scots rendered with cement margins and small windows.

Hillfoot Road

Narrow and steeply winding, note **The Aikars** (No 11), white 18th-century cottage distinguished by rolled skewputts; **Broomieknowe Cottage**, grander two-storey version, in whinstone; diminutive one door, one window, **Cashmere Cottage**; **Glenview**, whose basement was once a butcher's, and retains its ceiling meathooks and bottle glass windows; fine whinstone **The Broomieknowe** and **The Knowe**, early 19th century, with odd cherrycocking between larger pilastered doorway and hipped dormer windows.

The Tower, 1867, Peter Sinclair
Large Scottish baronial house, surrounded by tall
cypresses, entered through turreted tower
decorated with thistle-shaped motifs, finials and
ornate rope-design stringcourses. Old Muckhart
back road continues uphill, hillside now
dominated by rows of closely spaced speculative
housing, forming almost isolated commuter-
town, from mid-1960s, to accommodate
managerial staff from industrial Central Belt
attracted to the school – with little thought to
traffic implications for the old town.

Top *Former Hillfoot House, 1930s.*
Above and left *1993 Hillfoot House:*
rear elevation; front elevation.

Below *Hillfoot home farm.* Bottom
Castle Road.

Hillfoot House, 1993, Gavin Thomson
Previous 18th-century turreted house demolished
1980s following decades as roofless ruin. Estate,
which belonged to the Drysdales from at least 1569
until bought by the Moirs *c.*1800, landscaped and
planted with exotic trees many of which survive;
devastated in winter 2000–1. Fine walled garden
and ruinous coach house and old fountain base
remain. New house set into hillside just behind the
old site, using a geological fault in its base.
Contemporary and unobtrusive, using timber,
stone and slate to its advantage. Three-pointed star
plan provides eight levels, with views through and
sun at most times throughout the house; living
area spirals round triple fireplace chimney clad in
Locharbriggs sandstone (colour p.77).

Nearby, Hillfoot's **home farm** on Muckhart
back road includes gin-house (horse-mill);
sensibly converted to houses, 1997, Paul Edney.

Castle Road was the drove road through
Glenquey to Glendevon and Auchterarder, with
less adequate path through the hills to Blackford.
For many years the villages on either side of the
Ochils traded with each other via such hill roads.
No 1, late 18th century, built by Andrew Sharp as
his smithy and dwellinghouse. Little pyramid-
roofed structure nearby was the water

Blinkbonny by Jennifer Campbell.

association's filter house which served the Victorian waterworks; site now mostly redundant and requiring replacement with building of appropriate scale. **Blinkbonny**, 1797, the last cottage, set at an angle to the road, secluded within private garden, attractive whitewashed house with (later) attic dormers and plain margins, painted round windows, extended cleverly to rear, 1973, Colin Campbell. **No 19**, 1968, David Wallace, large L-plan brick house with flat roof, double-storey living room set into hillside below remainder of the accommodation.

Argyll Street

Last principal street of the Old Town, mostly redeveloped save for two small cottages and refaced **Lorne Tavern**. Convex-plan housing turning the corner from Argyll Street into **Sorley's Brae**, 1935, George Twigg of Thomas Frame and Son, for Dollar Town Council, with the council insisting on modification to original crescent layout. Sorley's Brae built by weaver (John Sorley), most notable being **Nos 14/16**, long, pantiled, late 18th-century, single-storey cottages.

Right *East Burnside.* Below *Argyll Cottage.*

East Burnside

A special feature of Dollar is the burn, its banks favourite sitting places of people resting on a summer's day, its verges and boulders ideal for children's nature studies and for guddling small trout. To each side of its cherry-tree-lined banks are fine late Georgian and Victorian cottages and villas (colour p.77). **Argyll Cottage**, *c.*1800 (No 6), Georgian-fronted cottage, attic with canted dormers, door surround splayed and front windows in unusual V-plan bays.

The Mylne or Middle Bridge

Flat segmented stone arch, reputedly built *c.*1820 to enable Revd Andrew Mylne, first rector of the Academy, to walk between school, church and manse (colour p.78).

108 Auld Kirk, 1775

Prominent on ridge above this delightful part of town sits the ruined gable and empty belfry of roofless Auld Kirk. It replaced a more ancient church on nearby site, from which came the 17th-century belfry. **Kirkyard** contains fine late 18th- and 19th-century memorials, older ones said to have been *borrowed* by the minister for supporting his hayricks in the nearby glebe. **Old Session House**, tiny 18th-century building in corner of kirkyard, sadly dilapidated, where kirk session met to decide on the school that changed Dollar's history.

109 Old Schoolhouse, 1780

Big rubble block with pantile roof and small gabled porch, upper floor added *c*.1800. Replaced original 1640 school and continued as parish school for the next century; now used as session house, re-roofed 1982. **Parish church hall**, large rectangular gothic church with broach spire, for United Presbyterians, 1876, Neil Macara, abandoned at unification with West United Free Church, Harviestoun Road, 1910.

West Burnside has a few late Georgian houses, ones nearer Bridge Street built with shops. Two bungalows at the top, first of a series of new houses on the Burnside, by local builder Tom Jack for himself and his sister, 1936–7. **Chapel Place**, formerly cul-de-sac off Cairnpark Street. **Park House**, dated 1822, fine Georgian house with Doric pilastered doorpiece and well-sculpted skewputts. Double house next door, **Mayfield**, formed from 1828 **Auld Secession Chapel**, from which the street is named. **Strathallan Hotel** opposite, two-storey rambling hotel and pub, began as St James' Hall or the Athenaeum.

Top *Auld Kirk and Old Session House.* Middle *Old Schoolhouse.* Above *Stone in kirkyard bearing the single legend:* this stone keeps to the dyke.

Left *West Burnside, 1904.* Below *Park House.*

Dollar Academy was founded on the munificence of a former herd boy from Dollar, John McNabb (b.1732), who became a wealthy sea captain resident in East London. He died in 1802 leaving half his fortune (worth £74,000 by 1818 whereas the original quote for building the school was £9,195), *for the endowment of a charity or school for the poor of the parish of Dollar* under the control of the Kirk Session. Such a scale of endowment to a parish of 670 souls caused considerable problems. It was always proposed to use the bequest for a school but Revd Watson wanted a boarding school whereas Craufurd Tait preferred a day school. Only after Watson died in 1815, and was replaced by the Revd Andrew Mylne, was the Institution (later Academy) determined upon. By 1843, it was the school which attracted attention, its 212 scholars (about a seventh of the entire population of the parish which had more than doubled in size since 1802) resulting from *the flocking of strangers to reside in the village for the sake of the excellent means of education it held out.* In 1853, Charles Roger noted that: *from its extreme rural quiet, few localities are better adapted than Dollar for youth prosecuting general study; while the picturesque scenery around, and great diversity in the surface of the land, singularly adapt it for the educational branches of drawing and mathematics. The attendance of pupils averages 350, of whom about 50 are boarders. Few institutions have supplied the country with so many teachers, and three professors have been appointed from amongst its masters to fill chairs in the Universities.*

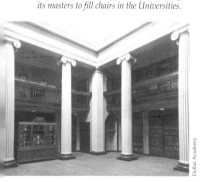

Right *Dollar Academy.* Above *The Playfair Library, c.1930.*

Turnpike and the Academy

In 1806, the new road from Kinross to Stirling offered the Taits of Harviestoun the chance of feuing large houses facing it. Some, built from the 1820s after Tait's insolvency, remain as **Bridge Street**. Focus of village dragged south; a new Dollar was in the making (letting the old one slumber away peacefully uphill), a more economic, enlightened 19th-century Dollar symbolised by the new Academy.

Playfair proposed to site the Academy south of Bridge Street, east of the burn, but Williamson's Meadow was preferred on the advice of John Hay (landscape) planner of Edinburgh.

Dollar Academy, 1818–20, W H Playfair (colour p.78)

The trustees appointed one of Scotland's finest architects and he responded by creating, on sloping ground to the west of the burn, an educational colony of a grandeur fully worthy of its dramatic setting. Splendid south-west facing façade of two storeys, dominated by giant pedimented portico at the head of a flight of steps, flanked by wings with attached columns, in Roman-Doric style normally symbolic of high-quality learning. Principal room was the splendid Greek-Ionic columned **library** – both portico and library reminiscent of his master William Stark's old Hunterian Museum in Glasgow – but library, along with rest of interior, lost in a fire in 1960. Interior recast, 1962, Watson, Salmond and Gray, in more utilitarian mould, creating three storeys where before there were two, gymnasium and school hall carved from 1866 John Burnet Sr wing at the rear. New buildings added to the policies.

In front is George Paulin's 1921 **war memorial** symbolising *Youth.* McNabb Street and Academy Place gates original, with West Approach added 1870s, south wall reduced and Cairnpark Street gates added 1907.

North of the frontage Law and Dunbar-Nasmith's competition-winning **Gibson Music Building**, opened 1991, by Sir Alexander Gibson, provides superb auditorium and practice rooms within low reflective glass-fronted pavilion, clad in sandstone, with sheeting roof (colour p.78). Later toilets in link corridor to Playfair building less successful. Music building now forms courtyard
110 with science block, now **Dewar Building**, 1910, Rowand Anderson & Paul, pleasant neoclassical block with projecting gabled entrance, extended 1953 and 1957. Behind, **Younger Building**, 1995, Law and Dunbar-Nasmith, for mathematics, business studies and information technology, linked to Dewar, 1998, when connecting corridors and attractive new glazed top floor and pitched roof added to 1950s' science extensions by McEachern MacDuff Architects.

Iona Building, 1996, McEachern MacDuff Architects, for Home Economics Department, squeezed out from Dewar Building, has made excellent re-use of previous music block, with new west-facing entrance and pitched roof.

Top *Section through Dollar Academy, original Playfair drawing.* Middle *Dewar Building.* Above *Younger Building.*

Gibson Music Building.

Sir James Dewar, 1842–1923, a native of Kincardine, was educated at Dollar Academy. His invention of the vacuum flask was necessary to his discovery (with Sir Fredrick Abel) of cordite. He is recollected by Dewar House and Dewar Street and by the Dewar Building at Dollar Academy.

The Science Building (now Dewar) was erected in the hopeful expectation of government money offered for the erection of school science buildings by a 1908 Act. Unfortunately it was later discovered that the Act only applied to Board Schools, so the academy had to bear the entire building cost of £6,000. Hence cuts. Nothing was *wasted on internal adornment, but nothing had been spared to make the internal fittings as complete and convenient as possible.* They could have done worse.

111 **Preparatory School**, 1937, William Kerr
Long classroom block with red tile hipped roof, lacking belfry lost in 1960s' fire, large windows to the south, clerestory lighting to the north, with three classrooms added at east end, 1997 and 1998. **Junior School**, 1888, Baldie and Tennant, as the Board School, colonised after new primary school built at Strathdevon. **Boys' Pavilion**, 1908, Hugh A Dalrymple, in white roughcast with red tile roof, fronted by huge loggia with balcony above.

Top *Gardener's Cottage*. Above
3 Academy Place. Right *Glenvar*.

Gateside, an ancient estate, has an old
charter stipulating the feuholder must
present a passing monarch with five
gallons each of old brewed ale, new
ale and ale in the process of brewing.
In the 18th century, it was the
principal inn on the old road. The
house brewed its own beer until early
19th century, with water from a spring
on Brewer's Knowe behind. The
brewhouse was on the site of the
present house, the stables where the
garage is and the two-storey inn on
Meadowbank's front lawn.

Below *Meadowbank*. Middle *Brooklyn*.
Bottom *28 Back Road*.

Behind the north Academy gate on Back Road
(formerly carriage entrance), heather-thatched
112 **Gardener's Cottage**, 1820, charming example of
small Georgian gatelodge with projecting
doorway, now with slate roof. Extended, 1994, as
new headquarters for Combined Cadet Force.

Academy Place, 1820–30, William Playfair
Six classical houses for the Academy, as masters'
accommodation, flanking original entrance from
the east. Ashlar fronted in Playfair's more rustic
Italianate vein, roofs hipped with shallow pitches,
the two western houses having central chimneys,
and overhanging eaves supported by modillion
brackets. Each door graced with triangular
pediment supported on unusual notched brackets.

Back Road
The Academy is bounded along its northern
perimeter by the old high road from Stirling to
Kinross, open to the hills beyond until enclosed
by 20th-century developments. **Glenvar** (No 4),
1906–8, William Kerr, unusual gabled villa of
harled brickwork, with steep double-gabled roofs
over tall bay windows, corner veranda and
conservatory reminiscent of English Arts &
Crafts. Arched recessed porch, tall stair oriel
window and tiny side round window make
impressive western entrance. Rented by Nepalese
prince, 1934–6, to the excitement of the village.
Meadowbank (No 8), 1934, also William Kerr
(similar to Glenvar in form), for the same family.

113 **Brooklyn**, *c.*1870
Large four-villa terrace of masters' houses, each
half-villa with projecting gable, cast-iron entrance
veranda and round-headed windows. **28 Back
Road**, 1960, Alastair Milne, intriguing and
unusual house in flat-roofed red brick.

114 **Thornbank Cottage**, mid-19th-century, gothic
villa with projecting gable and bay window.

Bridge Street
Clydesdale Bank, 7 Bridge Street, 1870s, probably William Railton
Typical Italianate banking palazzo, with triple and coupled windows, elaborate doorway, bracketed eaves and low hipped roof. One of the first villas feued by the Taits (or their trustees)

115 was **Homefield**, *c*.1822, fine house with droved ashlar front, architraved door enhanced by ornamental rosettes, a decoration repeated on other doors in the street. **Castle Campbell Hotel**, good solid coaching inn by the burn, from 1830s, still a pleasant place to stay.

116 **Rosevale**, 1820s
Symmetrical, well-proportioned windows with original glazing bars, central door flanked by pilasters, whole composition tied together by cornice at eaves line, well set off by tidy front

117 garden. **No 86**, another good example of 1820s' feuing, as is **Railway Tavern**.

Top *Dollar*. Middle *Bridge Street c.1920*. Above *Doorway, Homefield*.

Dewar House, previously an Academy boarding house (and formerly Aberdona Villa), and **Freshfield**, at corner of Devon Road, pair of 1850s' Tudor-gabled, double-villas, with neat gabled porches and ground floor bay windows. New house in Dewar's garden, 2001, Lomond Homes, responds well to the massing of original Bridge Street properties to its east and has superbly crafted stone frontage, let down by window proportions and door surround.

Freshfield.

Off Bridge Street, **Mitchell Court**, 1995–7, Keir and Fraser, justifiably award-winning development of housing for the elderly and for general needs built by the Miller Partnership and Ochil View Housing Association. Two-storey blocks gather round courtyards in former Burgh Yard, pink stone ground floors have cream harl above, window and door proportions and scale emulate those of early

Top and right *Mitchell Court*. Above *McNabb Street c.1900*.

Below *Dewar Street*. Middle *Former smithy, Campbell Street*. Bottom *Dollar Parish Church*.

20th-century architecture in the vicinity (see p.5 and colour p.79). Scottish Office Quality in Planning Award 1997 and NHTPC Partnership Award 1998.

Victorian Expansion
The obvious development after Bridge Street was built was to extend northwards towards the academy. **Cairnpark Street** developed first, feued by the academy in 1830s, comprises simple double-sided street of terraced cottages, forming pleasant group looking past the academy to the castle and hills. **Speedwell**, 13 McNabb Street, *c.*1820, simple classical house with low pitched roof, in the style of Playfair, decorated with wooden ornamental apron. **Heyworth** was Parkfield, built in 1868 for the academy's third rector, Revd Dr John Milne.

South of the Main Road
The opening of the railway in 1869 brought Stirling within 20 minutes reach, and the line to Kinross soon joined at Rumbling Bridge, opening up Dollar to the east. Old railway line – now a country walk – still forms the southern boundary of the town. **Station Road**, lower **McNabb Street** and **Devon Road** (main Dunfermline Road), all projected downwards from the main road and during the 1870s, '80s and '90s were built up with small, single-storey cottages. **Dewar Street**, forming the horizontal of the grid, has fine row of 1870s' cottages with canted dormers. Early 19th-century **smithy** in Campbell Street, now a house.

Strathdevon Primary School, 1964–5
Well-lit series of rectangular classroom blocks arranged around courtyards, now extended for new classrooms and given pitched roofs and enclosed porch. Hexagonal plan **Dollar Civic Centre**, 1996, next door in Park Place is a missed opportunity by Clackmannan District Architects to provide some contemporary excellence.

Muckhart Road
Dollar Parish Church, 1841, Sir William Tite Cruciform gothic, dominated by tall, battlemented

bell tower at south end; each roof corner has small corbelled angle turret with corbelled top. Choice of prominent London-based railway architect probably to do with Tite's being a board member of the Globe Insurance Company, which had taken over the Harviestoun Estate on Craufurd Tait's insolvency, and was therefore the parish heritor. Extended with rear gallery, 1862, side galleries, 1875, and rear chancel, new furnishings and organ by Rushworth and Dreaper, 1926. Stained glass by James Ballantyne & Son. Huge, rambling, old **manse**, St Columba's House, originally three-window house of 1795, enlarged for Revd Andrew Mylne, 1817. Tiny **kirkyard keeper's cottage**, *c.*1840, has central doorway with wooden porch and neat piended slate roof.

119   **Seberham**, *c.*1820, for the first writing master of the academy, with wide-eaved piended roof, canted dormer windows and unusually sculpted chimney shafts. **The Pines**, 1938, William Kerr

120 with Patrick McNeil, with Scots vernacular inspired detailing, an excellent example of the contemporary desire to be both modern and Scots. Simply projecting stairtower, Venetian bedroom window and elegant stone carved door form north-facing entrance.

The Ostlers, Kellybridge, 1988, Fiona Galbraith and Andrew Whalley
Small, special, energy-efficient, contemporary house in the form of square pyramid-roofed pavilion, with dressed sandstone walls to the road and to the west. Inside planned round central top-lit conservatory – a garden for bad weather – providing all circulation space (colour p.79). North and east walls fully glazed opening screens, sheltered by projecting roof and looking into very private garden contained by back walls of demolished Kellybridge Cottages (ostlers' accommodation for adjacent inn) and stables (still with aumbries for hay); while south wall continues along roadside as high rubble wall. Pioneering use in Scotland of transparent heated glazing system. Eric Lyons Housing Award Commendation, 1990, RIBA award, 1990.

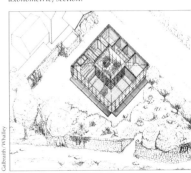

Top and above *The Pines: garden front in 1938; entrance front.*

Below and bottom *The Ostlers: axonometric; section.*

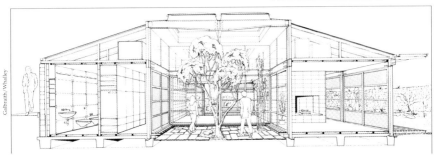

Top *Kellyside*. Above *Garden pavilion*.

121 Burnbrae Lodge, early 19th century
Built as The Oak Coaching Inn, distinguished by fine Doric-columned porch.

122 Kellyside, 1905, William Kerr
Large Arts & Crafts villa, similar to Dunmar (see p.51), with mock half-timbered gables and sweeping rosemary tile roof, screened from main road by dense hedging. Built by Clackmannanshire's Procurator Fiscal J B Haig, whose family had the Dollarfield estate (colour p.78). Open swimming pool with octagonal **garden pavilion** and timbered filter house, 1992, Matthew Pease, in matching red brick and rosemary tiles.

Harviestoun Road
Former Free Church, 1858, wings added 1864
Large gothic, later West United Free and then West Church, split into two houses after unification with parish church, 1975. Contains early example of laminated timber beams in roof structure, and incorporated rainwater downpipes within internal columns.

Jersey House, Henderson Place, 1876
A dog-tooth pattern brick villa built by manager of Dollar Brickworks as advertisement for his product lies under modern render. Formerly burgh offices and, until recently, local branch library.

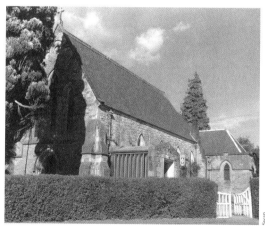

Right *St James the Great Episcopal Church*. Below *Rectory*.

123 St James the Great Episcopal Church, 1879–82, Adam Frame
Small nave and chancel in Early English gothic often adopted by Episcopalians as being nearer to their uncompromised roots. **Rectory,** built as Viewfield, *c*.1830, strictly classical with Doric-pilastered door and matching side wings.

Helen Place, *c*.1830

Three single-storey-and-basement houses round courtyard, middle house at rear faithfully restored. A refronting of late 18th-century brewer's house: simple ashlar cottage with hipped roof, window dressings picked out in white sandstone, wide raised door surround. Reputed to have been designed by Beattie & Armstrong of Edinburgh, builders of the academy.

Western Approach

Lined by neoclassical houses for the first masters who were learned and often wealthy scholars head-hunted to bring prestige to the academy. Houses are large, and masters supplemented their incomes by taking in boarders.

Woodcot, *c*.1820

Good example of late Georgian cottage: ashlar front, Doric-pilastered entrance flanked by windows, the arrangement of segmental fanlight and door sidelights identical to nearby Helen Place. In the parkland **Strachan Crescent**, 1957, Mactaggart & Mickel, perpetuates 1930s' details and imagery with corner windows.

124 **Springfield**, *c*.1830

Two-storey bay windows flank pilastered entrance; twin nearby, **Strathdevon**.

Top *Helen Place by Jennifer Campbell.* Above *Woodcot.*

Woodcot was built by Dr George Walker, an Englishman who settled in Dollar. He was a general practitioner and acquired the land on which he built Woodcot in March 1820. He was appointed physician to the Dollar Institution about 1827.

Devongrove.

125 **Devongrove**, 1821, possibly W H Playfair

Elegant mansion with projecting centre, screen side wings, hipped roof; segmented fanlight above entrance flanked by Doric pilasters, ground-floor windows within arched recesses like nearby **Birchgrove**, *c*.1750. Once outwith the town, Devongrove now flanked by 1990s' Wimpey housing.

126 **Broomrigg**, from 1804

Two-storey, stucco-faced Italianate, built by Craufurd Tait and enlarged when sold to James Leishman, *c*.1848, with double bow windows, balustraded, wall finials, parapet and double-

William Tennant, 1784–1848, is remembered as the author of *Anster Fair* (1812), the mock heroic poem describing his native Anstruther market. He came to Dollar in 1819 as the classics teacher and built Devongrove. A cripple from childhood, he *used two crutches and had a long walk daily to school.* In 1834 he left the academy to become Professor of Oriental Languages at St Mary's College, St Andrews. Captain Charles Gray, 1782–1851, expert on Scottish song, attempted to commemorate his co-founder of the *Anstruther Mousomanik Society* thus:

Thy river, clear winding, flows softly along,
Like the music of verse, or the notes of a song;
There the trout in his pastime glides swift
as a dart,
And oft cheats the angler, though crafty
his art;
There the tenants of nature at freedom
may rove,
No gun, net or link lurks in sweet
Devongrove.

Top *Fountain, Broomrigg.* Right *Broomrigg.* Above *Belmont, drawn by Jennifer Campbell, mid-19th-century red sandstone villa, continuing the series of large houses west along Harviestoun Road.*

columned porch. Mahogany fitted library built *c*.1900 by craftsmen from the then owner's shipyard on the Clyde. On roadside, mid-19th-century **fountain** – boy with pitcher within rock-faced dome. Original cast-iron boy now safe in Dollar Museum, his substitute a tinted concrete cast.

Mount Devon, 1827
Classical house, ground floor rusticated ashlar, with Doric-columned porch. Screen wings, added, 1847, complete the composition.

127 The Horseshoe
Previously Harviestoun Villa, a smithy in 1819, later reworked as Tudor cottage with central stone gable. Served as factor's house to Harviestoun estate.

Lower Mains
Hamlet comprising a few tidy cottages and neat council housing. Principal building is **Ochilton House**, Devon Road, 1831, with hexagonal porch, built by William Haig of Dollarfield.

128 Dollarfield
In 1787 William Haig founded commercial bleachworks along the north bank of the River Devon, to bleach cloth for the Dunfermline linen trade. He was among the first in Scotland to use sulphuric acid and then chlorine. He went on to assemble a large land holding, partly for bleachfields, partly for agriculture. The bleachworks lasted until 1937, became a sawmill and buildings demolished, 1963; site now caravan park. **Dollarfield House**, the Haigs' mansion, destroyed by a fire, 1940, replaced by modern farmhouse. Original steading, now considerably altered, once largest continuous lofted steading in Scotland. The dairy, or west range, hosts the small **Harviestoun Brewery**.

West Mill and its lade survives as bricked-up barn at West Haugh, alongside the Devon.

Across the bridge, **Rackmill** (or ford mill), grain mill in use about 1800, later electricity generator for the Haigs, converted to house, 1989.

Dollarbeg.

Dollarbeg, 1889, Ebenezer Simpson (colour p.79) Rambling, ornate red sandstone baronial mansion on ancient site high on south ridge above Dollar. Fruit salad of embellishment: corbelled turrets, crowstepped gables, moulded stringcourses, arched entrance porch and high four-storey entrance tower, similarly decorated. East wing restored as house for several families, but main house remains at risk. Contemporary stables and suitably turreted and crowstepped gatelodge.

Below *Solsgirth House*. Bottom *Loggia*.

Solsgirth House, from *c*.1870
Just over Perth and Kinross boundary, off Saline road, superb mansion has at its centre two-storey five-bay house, with French Gothic roof over entrance. Gradually 'stretched', first with ogival roofed three-stage tower and low crowstepped side range, which continued into faceted conservatory and long glasshouse or vinery. Enlarged again, 1898, with rear billiard room, with Art Nouveau fittings to library and north range – excellent leaded glass and lights. Side range then extended over conservatory to form superb huge ballroom (colour p.79) and gained a storey. Long colonnaded **loggia** replaced the vinery, and rather good service buildings to the rear include turreted former laundry. Superseded older house as home

to Wallaces and Sutherlands until 1930s, then to the Alexander (buses) family until 1980, then, after chequered existence as nursing home, from 1994 perfectly restored as family home and venue for weddings, conferences and idyllic holiday lets. **Solsgirth Farm**, behind, includes the earlier crowstepped house, dated 1722; openings under the harl show it was once three-storey but remodelled to provide two storeys with higher ceilings by the Victorians, extended, from 1994, by Matthew Pease. (For Saline see *The Kingdom of Fife* in this series.)

East of Dollar
129 **Kellybank**

Well-proportioned, early 19th-century farmhouse. In the 19th century coal mines and limekilns were developed here and at neighbouring Middleton. Traces of the steam engine and wheel on the Kelly Burn which drove Craufurd Tait's mine-shaft pump could long be seen.

Top *Art Nouveau light fitting, Solsgirth House.* Middle *Solsgirth Farm.* Above *Kellybank.*

Westerton.

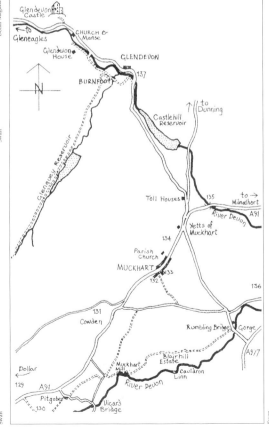

130 Westerton

Also known as Wester Pitgober, two adjoining farmhouses, east wing a two-storey rubble house, c.1790, and main house, c.1850, traditional three-window, two-storey block featuring semicircular **armorial panel** dated 1754 above the door. Arms are of John Ker, 5th Lord Bellenden of Broughton (1751–96) and may have been brought to Dollar from Broughton by later Kers when their estate was demolished for expansion of Edinburgh New Town in 1820s.

Top *Armorial panel, Westerton.* Above *Vicar's Bridge c.1900.* Left *Cowden Castle c.1950.*

Muckhart Mill, from 1666

Site of some building, and local grain mill powered by the Hole Burn, since 14th century, mill comprises three different rubble pantiled buildings set together at uneven angles. Main feature is cast-iron overshot waterwheel whose 20ft diameter makes it one of the largest in Scotland. **Mill house** and **steading**, 1780, tall, whitewashed, pantiled and much restored. Huge 35ft disused **limekiln**, with three arched openings, built into cliff face nearby and used by the Carron Company in mid-19th century. Ancient rubble **bridge** over the Hole Burn has a masonic evil eye to ward off unwelcome spirits.

Cowden Castle (demolished)

About 1320, Bishop William Lamberton of St Andrews (completer of the Cathedral) built a fortified palace known as Castleton. This continued as a mansion in some form or other, passing to the Earl of Argyll in 1491, then to the Gib family in the early 18th century, who built a second house, Easter Castleton, nearby. Neighbouring estate was called Cowden, owned by a branch of Bruce of Clackmannan from 1758. Mrs Bruce of Cowden, a widow (later Glen), augmented her estate with Easter Castleton in 1828, greatly extending the house and in 1834 also acquiring and demolishing

Vicar's Bridge

Early photographs show an enchanting single-arched bridge, entranced by its own reflection in the Devon, which collapsed in the 1950s and was replaced by a piece of modern utility.
A bridge was erected on this site in the 16th century. A 1765 plaque tells us *Thomas Forrest, who among other acts of charity, built this bridge.* Forrest was the *Good Vicar of Dollar,* a martyr of the Reformation who, choosing to preach by the Bible, was burnt for his beliefs in 1539 following his attendance at Thomas Cocklaw's wedding (see p.62). Forrest chose a beautiful setting for his bridge, to the advantage of the modern day picnic area, which was revitalised by Clackmannan District Council c.1985. An old oak tree nearby has the initials J B cut into its bark. In 1865 Joseph Bell attacked a baker travelling on the lonely road, was found guilty of murder and was given the last public execution in Scotland in Perth.

A number of mines and kilns left over from lime and ironstone workings of the early 19th century can be discovered in the locality of Vicar's Bridge. In 1830 the water draining out of one of the disused mine entrances was found to contain sufficient chemicals to be the attributed cure for a staggering number and variety of diseases.

From top: *Entrance hall, Cowden Castle, from Academy Architecture, 1907; octagonal turret and 16th-century archway; stables and Victorian arch; Cowden House.*

the Gib family's Wester Castleton. Ruins at Cowden therefore complicated and consist of octagonal **turret**, *c*.1800, with 1707 re-used lintel and 16th-century moulded **entrance arch**, both incorporated in *c*.1800 crenellated wall. Old **stables** nearby converted to house. Interesting Victorian **arch** leading to ruins topped by 18th-century bellcote with fluted pilasters and ball finial.

Castleton estate sold to John Christie, 1866, who renamed it Cowden Castle; house, enlarged and remodelled, 1893, Honeyman and Keppie (demolished 1952), reckoned to have incorporated early work by Charles Rennie Mackintosh – an octagonal tower with wrought-iron weather-vane, precursor of Glasgow Herald building tower (now The Lighthouse) begun the following year. Also, steel and wrought-iron suspension bridge on the estate, crossing the Devon near Arndean House, now being relocated to Naemoor Gardens by Matthew Pease, matches house extension railings in detail and incorporates gate screen with temptingly Mackintosh-like motif (see p.139). The entrance hall was remodelled, 1907, by H Ramsay Taylor to accommodate the teak stair that Ella Christie had made to her design and shipped from Burma (now in Tillicoultry Rugby Club). **Arndean House**, itself, pleasant early 19th-century mansion, in Perthshire, belonged to the Christies and is used by Christie descendants, the Stewarts, as principal estate house. **Cowden House**, on site of Cowden kitchen court, *c*.1966 bungalow with towers added, 1994, Matthew Pease, peeping through trees on the Cowden Bends.

131 **Japanese Garden**, 1907, Ella Christie and Taki Honda
Cowden was the lifelong home of Ella Christie, an intrepid traveller who journeyed to Europe, India, Tibet, China, Japan, Malaya, Burma, North Africa

Japanese Garden, 1950s.

and America. After visiting Japan in 1907, accompanying the Du Cane sisters, author and illustrator of *The Flowers and Gardens of Japan* (1908), she decided to transform a marshy field at Cowden into a Japanese garden. With the help of Taki Honda, a Japanese lady gardener, and the advice of Professor Susuki, Head of Soami School of Imperial Design (who thought it the *best garden in the western world)*, she laid out a lake surrounded by trees and shrubs, stepping stones and shrines with islands and bridges. Much frequented by Andrew Lang (1844–1912), poet, scholar, author and, above all, great eccentric, during his last years. There was also a visit from Queen Mary in 1932. From 1929, the garden had the caring attention of Mr Matsuo, a Japanese gardener who had lost all his family in an earthquake. Matsuo died in 1936 and is buried in Muckhart churchyard. Ella died in 1948 and the family was unable to maintain Cowden and the garden; nor was it able to interest anyone else. In the 1960s, shrines were vandalised, teahouses burnt down and new trees planted round about; fortunately many original trees survived and matured. One of few large-scale Japanese gardens in Britain, considered *one of the best*. Hopes continue for its restoration (colour p.80).

Middlehall, 1990, Matthew Pease
New house on hillside west of Muckhart resembling 16th-/17th-century L-plan tower house, fooling many into believing it is a historic landmark (colour p.80). In old farmyard, known as Middle Balliliesk in 18th century, harled and slated with stone doorcase; closer up the detailing (such as in the windows) is less convincing.

The leader of the Antiburgher section of the Scottish Secession Church, **Adam Gib**, 1714–88, came from Cowden (then known as Castleton). The Antiburghers (1747) believed it unlawful that city burgesses (magistrates) should have to take an oath to *the true religion presently professed within this realm*.

Middlehall.

Matthew Pease

POOL OF MUCKHART

Main Road, Pool of Muckhart.

Frequent winner of 'Scotland's best kept village' title for its flowing beds of colour and profusion of hanging baskets and window boxes, Muckhart guards the Glendevon pass through the Ochils to Perthshire from the counties of Kinross (to the

Above Christie coat of arms, Coronation Hall extension. Right *Coronation Hall.*

east), Fife (to the south) and Clackmannan (to the west). Outlying cottages, near the road junction, known as the 'Yetts of Muckhart' ('yett' meaning gate); the body of the village is the 'Pool'. Owes its existence to a drove road through the pass and, in the 19th century, it was common for at least every other cottage to become a hostelry around market time. Expanded little beyond original street of low stone cottages.

Below Melbreak. Middle *Pool Cottage.* Bottom *Datestone corbel, Pool Cottage, carved by Gillian Forbes.*

132 **Coronation Hall**, 1911, imported from the Glasgow Exhibition, white harled brick chamber, upgraded 2001 with lottery award. Extension, by Matthew Pease, pays homage to Ella Christie, who originally donated the land, and draws on Japanese design ideas, resets the Christie coat of arms stone from Cowden Castle in the entrance wall and provides Shinto gravel garden representing topography of the area.

South Dunlow and **Melbreak** form half-timbered English double villa with wide west-facing veranda, built for Ella Christie as staff accommodation, *c.*1904, possibly William Kerr. Original name Dungloe apparently suggested by Sir Robert Lorimer (then extending Briglands, across the Devon), but rejected by later owners as unfortunate prefix to 'Muckhart'. Nearby houses, in School Road, typical 1950s' county architect cottages; two steep-roofed double houses, 1946, Ian Moodie, clad in vertical boarding, in Swedish style, just as charming. **Pool Cottage**, at junction of old and new roads, with bold new extension, 2001, Matthew Pease, built out into the road, acting as visual stop.

133 **Holestone**, previously Hollytree Lodge and Astral Villa (name changes every 50 years), grander, with its tripartite doorway and fanlight, repeated inside in stone-flagged entrance hall, similar to houses on the outskirts of Dollar, but with additions to the east, its perfection slightly marred by a dormer window.

The Inn, 1806, double white-rendered cottage with black margins, generally typical of Muckhart cottages; wooden oriel windows a modern touch, but go well with the picturesqueness of the village. Cottages along **Main Road** all date from around early 1800s, each delighting in an Arcadian name: Ochil House, Woodend, Hillview and Ivy Cottage.

Parish Church, 1838
Simple rubble chamber with small square bellcote and fine Georgian arched windows; original woodwork in pews and west gallery. Set into east gable are four date stones representing previous churches on the site: 1620, 1699, 1713 and 1789, above memorial to the Christies of Cowden. Nearby **manse**, 1832–4, William Stirling, fairly plain, traditional, two storey with long low west wing.

Top *Seamab Villa, 18th-century two-storey cottage on Main Road.*

Balliliesk.

YETTS OF MUCKHART

134 **Balliliesk**, from *c*.1835
On older site – Patons lived here in 16th century. Large two-storey house, with round-headed windows and squat Italianate tower for library, with custom-built bookcases added *c*.1862, when interiors redesigned. May have replaced north pavilion of now asymmetrical west front; windows show evidence of removed lying panes. New kitchen wing added, 1998, Matthew Pease, in keeping with the original; walled garden and related offices. **Ellislea**, late 18th century, once the Yetts Inn, then Royal Hotel, good house with fine rectangular fanlight, quoins and door dressings unusually finished with bold rustication.

Former **East Manse**, *c*.1740, two-storey three-bay house, with later north wing, for the minister of the Secessionist Church (demolished) established when the unpopular Revd Archibald Rennie was imposed on the village with the aid of the army. The parish church lay empty for 52 years!

East Manse.

Devonhall.

Below *Caplawhead*. Middle *Mosspark*.
Bottom *Stable/motor house*.

On 6th July 1699, Robert Livingstone, chapman at Crook of Devon, pleaded guilty to stealing a black tup and two wedder sheep, and was sentenced *to be stripped naked of his clothes, and scourged by the hand of the hangman through the whole town of Clackmannan with one of the sheep's heads and four feet hanging about his neck, and thereafter to be banished out of the said shire.*

Devonhall, 1903

Fine Italianate villa for William Harley, a Kirkcaldy ironfounder, on East Manse glebe, walls smooth-rendered in ochre, topped by wide frieze decorated with anthemia (colour p.80). Red-tiled hipped roof has wide overhanging eaves and matching dormers to attic rooms. South front has projecting columned veranda with balcony above; splendid gardener's garden.

Caplawhead

Low farmhouse dated 1837 with initials WF and JMcN, appropriately extended with new stone dormers and Lorimeresque corner tower, 1994, Matthew Pease, for the son of the late Ian G Lindsay. Until 1933 the feuholder was required to supply the Duke of Argyll with transportation of wine, a supply of lime for repairs to Castle Campbell and the provision of eight mounted lancers and four carriage horses.

Mosspark (formerly Nether Moss farmhouse), from *c.*1780

Originally two-storey three-bay house, remodelled 1906 for Dr Grace Caddell, one of Scotland's first women GPs, involved in setting up the Elsie Inglis Hospital, Edinburgh, and in raising foster children here. Tall conical roofed tower added behind for the plumbing, and attic storey in French Renaissance style. Delightful crowstepped brick and harled **stable/motor house**, *c.*1906, possibly William Kerr, requires repairing after a fire.

Fossoway

Ancient parish now largely made up of the villages of **Drum** and **Crook of Devon** in Kinross-shire (see *Perth & Kinross* in this series).

135 **North Fossoway Bridge**, carrying Milnathort road over the River Devon, single segmental arch of great antiquity, repaired 1780 and 1882 – the date it bears.

136 Lendrickmuir, 1874, Adam Frame
Impressive, unorthodox, neoclassical mansion,
built as Naemoor House for Robert Moubray of
Cambus Distillery, interior includes very
elaborate plasterwork. Now Scripture Union
retreat, good stable block at entrance retained as
classrooms. **Naemoor Gardens**, intended group
of four new houses by Matthew Pease in former
brick walled garden across the road, backing onto
the Devon. Only **Vinea**, 2000, built so far, the best
new house in the Muckhart area, with pea plants
and pods carved on stone entrance lintel by
Gillian Forbes as playful pun on the architect-
developer's name. Cowden iron bridge, possibly
by Mackintosh (see p.134), being relocated here,
on axis visually linking Adam Frame's handsome
stone pedimented doorcase in garden wall and
Sir Robert Lorimer's 1908 Briglands Lodge to the
south to give residents access to public walkway
being created on south bank.

Lendrickmuir.

Lord Abercromby directed the
Highland Society to Clackmannanshire
after 1819, introducing draining of fields
instead of fallowing. The first premium
offered was gained by John Moubray, of
Cambus Distillery, where he developed
his distillery. His skills were put to use
elsewhere, for Moubray had bought a
bog at the eastern extremity of
Clackmannanshire in 1820 and spent
large sums of money draining it, the
joke being that, after which, there was
'nae moor nae more', hence the name
Naemoor House.

Left *Vinea.* Below and bottom:
*Rumbling Bridge Nursing Home; panel
commemorating the two dates of the bridge.*

Rumbling Bridge and **Devon Gorge**
Beside Old Coaching Inn, *c.*1820, extended *c.*1835
and now **Rumbling Bridge Nursing Home**, is
one of the most beautiful stretches of the River
Devon. Railway to Kinross opened, 1863, with
celebratory dinner in the upgraded 'hotel'. Good
exercise in Gothic Revival, probably dating from
railway's arrival, including heavily timbered
gables and two Puginian doorcases; huge
extension, 1999, James Denholm, towers over the
gorge. Gardens were particularly splendid, with
topiary. Nearby buildings included Indian
bungalow (now antique shop), half-timbered post
office, another half-timbered double villa and
English-style stone Arts & Crafts house, which,
with gothic hotel and castellated bridge,
contributed to the appeal of the gorge as
Victorian tourist resort.

RUMBLING BRIDGE

Rumbling Bridge c.1900.

At **Rumbling Bridge** the water has cut deep through the landscape to form gorges, pools and waterfalls. As the taste for romantic experience grew, the Devon Gorge was added to the list of sights. In 1769 Thomas Pennant made a detour to admire *the large and deep cylindrical cavities like cauldrons. One in particular has the appearance of a vast brewing vessel; and the water, by its great agitation, has acquired a yellow scum exactly resembling the yeasty working of a malt liquor.* Sarah Murray, in 1798, advised all travellers to divert for the thrill and, in the 19th century, they did. Coaches travelling from Edinburgh to the Highlands made regular stops at Rumbling Bridge Hotel. In 1871 the road was joined by the **Devon Valley Railway** providing five of the most beautiful miles of railway in the country, under and over 17 bridges and a viaduct, close to the banks of the river. **Rumbling Bridge Station**, to which visitors flocked in their thousands, survives as housing.

MacEachin's Cave, below Devil's Mill, is named after a Jacobite romance. A young soldier, Hector MacEachin, had been imprisoned in nearby Castle Campbell, but was rescued by Hannah Haig, daughter of the laird of nearby Blairhill, and hidden in the cave at the Devon Gorge. Hector later rejoined his army but was again imprisoned after the defeat of the '45. He escaped execution at Carlisle by a legal slip-up, and returned to marry Hannah.

Cauldron Linn c.1880.

Rumbling Bridge, 1713 and 1816
Old lower bridge, built by William Gray, was only 12ft wide without parapets … *the want of a parapet prevents even the steadiest head from looking down this frightful chasm, without a degree of terror* (Dr Garnett, 1798). The 1816 bridge above was superimposed creating an unusual double bridge. Viewed from below, it is a spectacular sight, and the reverberating sounds of the river forcing its way through the rocks explain its name. Upstream, **Devil's Mill**, loudest of the cascades producing noise like running machinery, never ceases even on the Sabbath; thus earning its title. The celebrated **walks** have been re-opened with new bridges, gates and access points.

Cauldron Linn
Said to be one of the finest waterfalls in Scotland, and a famous beauty spot long before Dr Garnett, in 1798, described in great detail his visit to Cauldron Linn, Rumbling Bridge and Devil's Mill. Between two falls, which together total about 90ft, are three deep pools, or linns, gouged out of the rock. Water flows through holes under the surface, and the froth makes each pool resemble witches' cauldrons. Water in the cylindrical intermediate pool is constantly swirling and must be the cauldron in question. Small-scale hydro-electric scheme installed, 1927, to light Blairhill mansion house above, replaced, 1993, Matthew Pease, with a system that now supplies enough power for Muckhart and Crook of Devon, the pipe buried this time to respect the view. Of **Blairhill**, an estate linked to the Haig whisky family (cousins of the

Dollarfield Haigs), only significant survivors are former dower house, which has a little Georgian plasterwork, and the pyramid roofed lodge at Rumbling Bridge; immense walled garden repossessed by nature and small family shrine shrouded in dense woodland. Gardener's cottage fell over the cliff and has been replaced.

Smithy House, *c.*1835
Smithy probably served the hotel and its coaches; latterly petrol filling station, refurbished and enlarged 1991, Matthew Pease. Wheelwright's and joiner's shops also restored. The K6 telephone kiosk looks the part, but came from Drumchapel and contains a stuffed bear.

Up Glendevon Road, two former **tollhouses** flank each side by the Dunning junction. Eastern one unaltered: three windows, with broad-eaved, hipped roof and centre chimney, seriously at risk.
  Castlehill Reservoir, on the River Devon, flooded the valley. **St Serf's Bridge**, or Roman Bridge, ancient single arch with, some say, monastic carvings below, was the loss. There may have been a Roman camp at the head of the dam.

Robert Burns visited Harviestoun on at least two occasions during 1787, to see his friend Gavin Hamilton. Burns recorded: *After breakfast we made a party to go and see the Cauldron Linn: a remarkable cascade in the Devon about five miles from Harviestoun; and after spending one of the most pleasant days I ever had in my life, I returned to Stirling in the evening.* Burns' pleasure was probably caused by Mrs Hamilton's daughter Charlotte, for whom Burns wrote his poem *The Banks of the Devon:*

> *How pleasant the banks of the clear winding Devon,*
> *With green-spreading bushes, and flow'rs blooming fair!*
> *But the bonniest flow'r on the banks of the Devon*
> *Was once a sweet bud on the braes of the Ayr.*
> *Let Bourbon exult in his gay, gilded Lilies,*
> *And England triumphant display her proud Rose,*
> *A fairer than either adorns the green vallies*
> *Where Devon, sweet Devon, meandering flows.*

Left *Smithy House.* Below *St Serf's Bridge c.1920.* Bottom *Castlehill Reservoir.*

Right *Glentower House.* Top *Entrance arch, Glentower House.* Above *Tigh-na-Greinne with campanile of Glentower House behind.*

Glendevon

The general aspect is hilly, but the hills are green and smooth, seldom incumbered with rocks, and only a few spots are covered with heath … The windings of the river, the plantations with which it is skirted, and the surrounding scenery, form a highly picturesque prospect, wrote William Chalmers in 1803, and still true today.

Across stone arched **Black Linn Bridge**, 1836, James Mitchell, engineer, and James Buchan, builder (over another celebrated pool in the Devon), is **Glentower House**, former Castle Hotel stripped of Edwardian castellations and now, behind the great **entrance arch**, returned to the simple villa with Italianate campanile built by the Bald Harveys in 1880, Victorian owners of Carsebridge Distillery. Original cottage which they extended also survives. **Tigh-na-Greinne**, to the west, conceived and developed by Alastair Stewart of Survair Services, detailed,

137

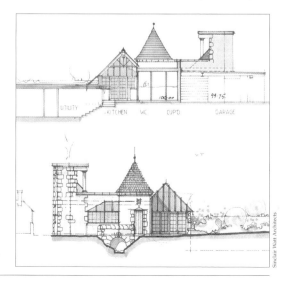

Section showing proposed addition to Tigh-na-Greinne.

142

1989, by I D MacDowall, low, grass-roofed, glass-fronted house, set semi-underground into hillside and enjoying all-day sunshine and spectacular river views. Intended addition, 2001, Sinclair Watt Architects, will combine bedrooms on east side into separate, new, split-level house over a burn and incorporate little tower left over from the hotel, previously balcony for upper-floor bedrooms.

Tormaukin Hotel, 19th-century coaching inn, with memories of sheep droving days; popular in 1890s with anglers: *a convenient and opportune resting place for the not wearied, but – with the scenery – enchanted traveller.* Still a hotel and, now with enlarged restaurant, an ideal stopping place.

Tormaukin Hotel.

Borland, on hill behind, two-storey farmhouse, recast from 18th-century house with 1765 initialled stone of David Law and Catherine Rutherford, and 1747 stone on the steadings.

Left *Burnfoot bridge and cottages in 1986.* Below from top *Stables, Burnfoot; arched gateway to Glendevon House; 1766 panel on gateway; Glendevon House.*

Burnfoot

Former weaving hamlet on other side of river by Glenquey Burn, survived by a few stone cottages and sturdy arched 18th-century bridge. The 19th-century wool-spinning mill has gone and long-deserted cottages now reclaimed, **stables** being particularly attractive example, with contemporary wrought metalwork to external stair. Two-storey harled **Glenquey** farmhouse, up the glen, has 17th-century marriage lintel.

Glendevon House, 1818, probably James Gillespie Graham (or possibly W H Playfair) Very fine neo-Tudor cottage house, for Rutherfords of Glendevon Castle (dated *R 1818* inside), with low-pitched broad-eaved roof and fine interior, built onto 1762 house, now gone. Approach over 1757 double-arched bridge; arched **gateway** contemporary with the house re-uses 1766 **panel** associated with the castle,

143

GLENDEVON

Gallows Knowe, the name of the hill behind Glendevon House, commemorates the execution of 14 men there in one day.

Top and right: *Glendevon Church.*
Above *Tarmangie House.*

Right *Glendevon Castle c.1920.*
Below *Glendevon Castle from rear.*

adjoining lodge by the river. **Glendevon Church**, simple mid-18th-century whitewashed chamber with five windows, square stone bellcote and plain slate roof: who could want more in these beautiful surroundings? Added to in 1803 (dated), altered 1846 and reseated, 1886, by Adam Frame. Overshadowing church is **Tarmangie House**, immense former manse, 1747, with dormered second floor, 1896, James Mitchell, and piend-roofed porch, 1913, William Kerr.

Glendevon Castle, 15th century onwards Formerly Z-plan, only four-storey south tower survives to full height, north tower and main block reduced in height and considerably altered. First castle on the site belonged to the Douglas family in the 15th century, from which part of massive central block may date, extended early 17th century, possibly when it passed to the Rutherfords. Lean-to at the east built in 1966. Still in occasional seasonal use as public house associated with nearby caravan park.

Up the glen, **Kaimknowe**, 18th-century bow-ended farmhouse, extended and refitted internally *c.*1840. **Wester Glen Sherup**, near summit, re-uses old two-storey house as outbuildings, dated 1693, and 1694 on its own outbuildings. **Whitens**, 1887, nearby, re-uses 1684 marriage stone. At the summit is the source of the Devon and our journey is complete. Over the hill is **Gleneagles** (see *Perth & Kinross* in this series).

This revised edition takes the 1987 guide as its starting point and so I would like to again thank everyone who helped with the original book: especially Charles McKean who enhanced and edited the text and Stewart Fowler who assisted throughout the project; David Walker, Robert Rankine, Jean Peacock, Murray Dickie, Ronald Hunter, Duncan Stirling, the late Bill Bracewell, Vicki Bryant, Alex McLaren, Isobel Drummond, Rena Cowper, Isobel Grant Stewart, the late Mary Kerr, Tony Martin, David Graham, Jennifer Campbell, the late Tom Jack, Peter Allam, Alan Wightman, Lord Balfour of Burleigh, David Hynd, Alison Bryce (née Ewart), Catherine Schroder and Tayona McKeown.

The new edition could not have happened without the support of Andrew Millar and Keir Bloomer of Clackmannanshire Council, who have assisted throughout, Helen Leng and Susan Skinner of the Rutland Press, who have both been amazing in shaping the guide at every stage, or Adrian Hallam of the Almond Consultancy whose considerable design talents created the finished volume. I am particularly indebted (again) to Charles McKean and David Walker, to Robert Rankine who has contributed to numerous entries, to Jennifer Campbell, Duncan Stirling and David Graham all of Dollar, and to Susan Mills of Clackmannanshire Council's excellent Museum and Heritage Services, Matthew Pease, Janet Carolan of Dollar Museum, Bruce Baillie, Ken Tullis and Gordon Roger, all of whom commented on versions of the new text. Many others helped with invaluable pieces of information. Yvonne Gray scanned the original text and my family have been a tremendous support: the late Sheila Swan, John Swan, Richard Swan, Cate Stevens and Andrew Rourke.

BIBLIOGRAPHY

Adamson, J: *A Glimpse into the Past of Sauchie and Alloa*, 1981; Archibald, J: *Alloa Sixty Years Ago*, 1911; Baillie, B: *History of Dollar*, 1998; Billings, R W: *The Baronial and Ecclesiastical Architecture of Scotland*, 1852; Brown, W C: *Clackmannanshire, A Guide to Historical Sources*, 1984; Chalmers, W: *The Gazetteer of Scotland*, 1803; Lord Cockburn: *Circuit Journeys*, 1888; Colvin, H: *A Biographical Dictionary of British Architects 1600–1840*, 1995 edition; Cowper, A S: *Sidelights on Alva History*, 1972; Crawford, J: *Memorials of the Town and Parish of Alloa*, 1874; Crouther Gordon, T: *The History of Clackmannan*, 1936, *A Short History of Alloa*, 1937; Defoe, D: *A Tour Through the Whole Island of Great Britain*, Furbank and Owens edition, 1991; *The Dictionary of National Biography; The Dollar Magazine*, from 1902; Dollar Civic Trust: *Chap Book*, 1977; Drummond, A I R: *Old Clackmannanshire*, 1953, unpublished thesis: *The Castellated and Domestic Architecture of Clackmannanshire and its Borders from the Mediaeval Period to the Year 1830*; Evans, E J: *Tillicoultry, a Centenary History*, 1972; Gall, A: *Popular Tour Round the Ochils*, 1893; Gibson, W: *Reminiscences of Dollar, Tillicoultry, Etc*, 1883; Groome, F H: *Ordnance Gazeteer of Scotland*, 1882–85; Historic Scotland: *Descriptive Lists of Buildings of Architectural and Historic Interest – Clackmannanshire*; Hume J R: *The Industrial Archaeology of Scotland*, 1976; Hume-Brown, P: *Early Travellers in Scotland*, 1891; Johnston, T & Tullis, R: *Muckhart*, 1989; Kelsall, R: *A Blairlogie Boyhood*, 1999; Kirk, R: *Historical Sketch of Tullibody*, 1890 and 1937; Lothian, J: *Alloa and its Environs*, 1861; MacGibbon & Ross: *The Castellated and Domestic Architecture of Scotland*, 1887–92; McMaster, C: *Alloa Ale*, 1985; Park, B A: *The Woollen Mill Buildings in the Hillfoots Area*, 1979; Ramsay, J: *Scotland and Scotsmen in the 18th Century*, Allardyce edition, 1888; RCAHMS: *Well Sheltered and Watered: Menstrie Glen, a farming landscape near Stirling*, 2001; Roger, C: *A Week in Bridge of Allan*, 1853; Scott, W: *Waverley*, 1885 edition; Wallace, J: *The Sheriffdom of Clackmannan*, 1890; Watt, L: *Alloa and Tullibody*, 1902; The First, Second and Third, *Statistical Accounts*.

Clackmannanshire Council and its predecessor District Council Libraries have published an excellent series of old and new local works of which it is possible to acknowledge only the more significant. A useful source of information was the local collection of books, pamphlets, letters, photographs and microfilm copies and indices of newspapers held at Alloa Library, and the support of David Hynd and Ian Murray is much appreciated.

PHOTOGRAPHS
The source of each photograph is credited alongside. Particular thanks are due to Stewart Fowler, Alex McLaren, Anne Ferguson, the Royal Commission on the Ancient and Historical Monuments of Scotland, and Clackmannanshire Council for original photographs and illustrations – their production owed much to White House Studios. The new edition incorporates many new photographs by Andrew Millar, Clackmannanshire Council and especially freelance photographer Bill Robertson. Thanks also to Alex Shuttleworth, Robert Rankine and contributors to the *Wee County Picture Roadshow*, an invaluable digitised archive of historic local photographs. Paintings by David Allan are reproduced by kind permission of the Earl of Mar and Kellie, the Earl of Cathcart, and the University of Dundee. Other original artworks are reproduced by kind permission of the artists: Jennifer Campbell, Oscar Goodall, Lys Hansen and Adam Robson.

INDEX

James Stobie's map of Clackmannanshire in 1783.

Dollar Academy

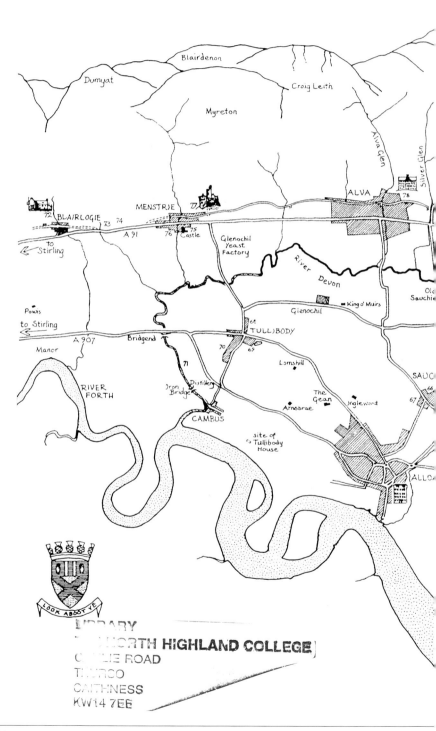

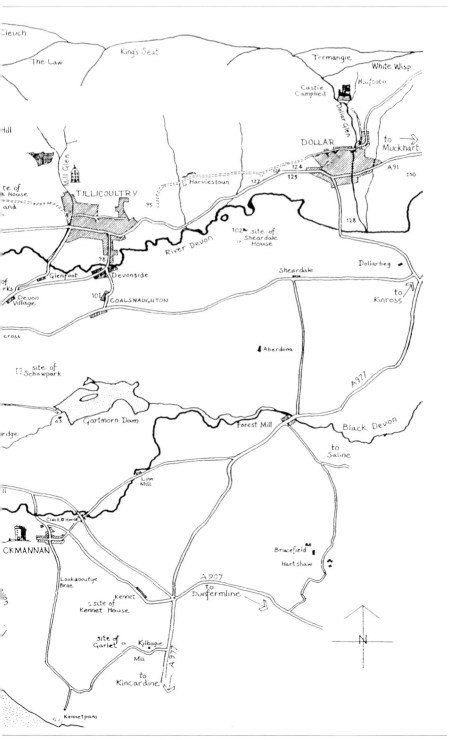

151

GLOSSARY

1. Ashlar (dressed stonework in smooth blocks).
2. Balustrade (line of small columns usually along a balcony or parapet – in this case in ironwork.
3. Bow (projecting semicircular bay).
4. Buttress (stone column supporting the walls, usually of a church).
5. Cherrycocking (small stones set between larger blocks of stone).
6. Corbel (stone supporting a projection above, one end embedded into the wall).
7. Cornice (projecting top of a wall).
8. Crowstepped gable (a gable in the form of a series of steps).
9. Curvilinear gable (wavy).
10. Cupola (roof light).
11. Dormer window (window projecting through the roof plane).
12. Drum tower (circular one-bay tower, usually for staircase).
13. Eaves (overhanging edge of a roof).
14. Fanlight (patterned glazed window above a door).
15. Finial (crowning feature in this case, of a tower).
16. Keystone (centre stone of an arch).
17. Palazzo (a building in imitation of an Italian Renaissance palace).
18. Pavilion roof (piended, or hipped – sloping on all four sides).
19. Pediment (triangular feature).
20. Pilaster (flattened column attached to a wall).
21. Quoin (long and short protuberant stones emphasising the corner).
22. Stringcourse (stone course or moulding projecting from the surface of the wall).
23. Tracery (window pattern, usually in churches).
24. Venetian window (three-part window, the centrepiece raised and curved).
25. Wallhead or nepus gable (gable rising through the roof in the front of a building).

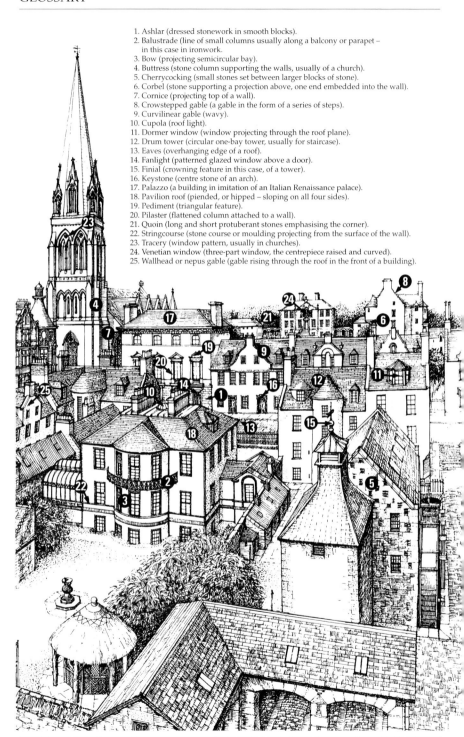